Walks around Reeth & Upper Swaledale

By

Keven Shevels

First published in Great Britain in 2012 by Trailguides Limited.
www.trailguides.co.uk

ISBN 978-1-905444-52-6

The route diagrams in this book are based upon 1925-1940 Ordnance Survey One-Inch maps updated by field trips and site visits.

Trailguides Limited
35 Carmel Road South
Darlington
Co Durham DL3 8DQ

Cover design by Steve Gustard.

CONTENTS

Cover photos.
Front. Standing at the remains of the smelt mill chimney. Walk 8: Grinton How Smelt Mill & the Grovebeck Mines. Back cover. The Bronze Age co-axial wall on Calver Hill. Walk 5: The Settlements of Calver.

INTRODUCTION

1. Introduction

Considered to be the capital of Upper Swaledale, Reeth lies at the point where Arkengarthdale joins the main valley of the Swale. Sitting as it does on a platform above the confluence of the two water courses, the Arkle Beck and the River Swale, this dales village is dominated by the high fells surrounding it, with the dramatic scars and cliffs of Fremington Edge looming to the east, the heights of Calver Hill rising up behind the houses to the west and the bulk of Harkerside to the south.

With it's location, it was natural that Reeth would develop as a trading centre but with the industrialisation of the lead mining industry during the 18th and 19th centuries the village rapidly grew as the hub of mining within the dale. At it's height during the early 1800's the village boasted a population of 1,460, three times the size of what it is today and around the green existed over thirty shops plus a weekly market.

But the lead industry is a fickle mistress and by the end of the 1800's the collapse of the market price of lead closed the majority of the mines in the dale with only one or two surviving into the early 1900's. Virtually within the space

The footbridge over the Swale.

The swing bridge below Reeth was built in 2002 replacing an earlier one that was swept away by floods. The first bridge was built in 1920 after the community raised the funds to link the parishes of Grinton and Reeth, the previous method of crossing the river being a set of stepping stones from one bank to the other. This first bridge stood for 80 years and withstood a number of major floods until the night of 19 September 2000 when it finally succumbed to one of the regular spates that occur on this river.

of a couple of years, an industry that had existed and given employment to thousands within the valley for over two centuries ended in mass unemployment. However, people have to eat and live and both Reeth and the wider dale depopulated as the desperate workers left for employment in the coal mines of the North East or the mills of Lancashire, many even seeking new lives abroad.

Today the area relies on agriculture, which was always a fundamental part of the economy even in the halcyon days of mining, and the ever growing rise of tourism. There is no doubt that the natural beauty of Swaledale attracts the visitor, especially the walker keen to sample some of the most spectacular landscapes in England.

For the walker, Reeth can be described as almost perfect. Here the surrounding hills and moors provide a landscape littered with a legacy of the past. Four thousand years of history can be explored by the walker, ranging from prehistoric earthworks and settlements, Iron Age hill forts, the fortifications bordering Dark Age Kingdoms, Medieval religious houses and extensive lead mine remains.

2. Access & the Right to Roam

As you'll see from the walks, the area around Reeth has been inhabited since the earliest days and many of the footpaths and bridleways surrounding the village date back over many generations, reflecting the routes that have been historically used for communication between the villages and hamlets of the dale and also for work, to travel to and from the distant mines and other places of labour.

In the cultivated areas, namely the valley floor and the sides of the dale, access is restricted to the public rights of way that form quite a comprehensive network around the village. The vast majority of these routes are very well marked with marker posts and markers on gates and stiles. Most are quite well used and easily followed on the ground.

Compared to the usage of these rights of way, the freedom of access that was granted under the Countryside Rights of Way Act (CRoW) 2000 in 2005 is comparatively recent, this opens up the high ground and moors above the valley to the walker and gives the 'right to roam'. A right that should not be underestimated.

With the implementation of this Act the majority of the upland areas of Swaledale have now become legally accessible. The legislation allows walkers the right to roam at will over "designated access land" without the need to be restricted to official footpaths and bridleways. On the new editions of the Ordnance Survey Explorer maps, this new access land is marked with a light yellow coloured background and at the entry points to this land, the stiles and gates carry the new "access land" waymarking symbol of a brown stick man in a brown circle.

With the right to access has also come responsibility and the walker is expected to observe various limits and restrictions that are placed on their activities at certain times of the year. The landowner and/or farmer has the right to exclude access for up to twenty eight days per year and this normally applies between May and early July coinciding with the breeding season of the ground-nesting birds on the moors. Where they are known, any restrictions that may impinge on the given walk are shown in the details for that walk. However, don't take it for granted that these are going to be accurate. Every year circumstances can and do change and restrictions may alter, always check any notices that are placed at the access points for restrictions. Further information on both access and general and specific restrictions can be found on the website **www.countrysideaccess.gov.uk**

3. The Walks

The nine walks in this book have all been designed to showcase that area of Swaledale that surrounds the village of Reeth and as such most of them use the village green as their starting and finishing point. However, note that the Harkerside and Apedale walk does start and finish just outside Grinton.

As usual when I base any of my books on a particular location I like to include a mix of walks of varying types and distances, so within this selection you will find river bank and field path walks, moorland walks and even one that crosses the high watershed between Swaledale and Wensleydale. I try to suit all possible tastes but at the same time present walks that are, maybe, not quite so obvious.

Most of the walks in this book start and finish at the village green in Reeth which is central to the village. This is also the main site for visitor parking although at busy times during the summer this area can become quite full, illustrating the popularity of this village.

As with any collection of walks that start and finish from the same location, there are always going to be a limit on the number of ways in and out of Reeth. As a result you will find that some of the walks do have a slight duplication of their route in their early and finishing stages but as far as possible this has been kept to a minimum.

Anybody who has used one of my books before will realise that I have a little bit of a passion for history and how this is reflected in the landscape. As always this is shown within these walks as I quite frequently used them to visit and explore certain aspects of the countryside that I, personally, find quite interesting. I don't believe that walking guidebooks should be boring and, hopefully, the walks and associated notes will help convey my enthusiasm for the valley of Swaledale to you both as a reader and as a walker.

In the details preceding each of the walks there is an approximate time taken for that particular walk which includes a reasonable time to explore the various sites of interest that are visited. However, this can be variable depending upon how long you, as the walker, take to explore these sites. If you chose not to have a look and investigate then the time taken will obviously be shorter whereas if you linger and have a good mooch about then you may be longer than I have estimated.

With the huge impact that lead mining had on the dale, it is perhaps inevitable that a number of these walks pass old lead mines and workings and with some of the routes these are actually a feature of the walk. However, resist any temp-

Rainbow over Fremington Edge.

tation to enter and explore these openings as it is extremely dangerous to do so. It is over one hundred years since these mines were abandoned and during the intervening period there has been no maintenance work carried out in them with the result that both rot and erosion has taken it's toll and many of these levels are no longer stable.

The walks in this book have all been graded in accordance with the Ferguson Grading System (`FGS`) and the actual grading is set out at the beginning of each individual walk to help you assess their difficulty. A detailed explanation of the FGS and how individual gradings are determined is set out on pages 107-109 in the Appendix to this book.

4. The Weather

Reeth lies in the middle of Upper Swaledale and is surrounded by the high hills of the North Pennines. Here the weather can be very changeable even during summer and the exposed altitude of this area can make even a balmy summer's day seem cold and uninviting. Mist and low cloud can be experienced no matter the time of year and at times this can roll in quite quickly catching the walker unaware and heavy localised rain is also not uncommon. Don't misjudge these moors, although due to global warming the heavy snow falls of yesterday aren't as regular as they once were, they do still happen. No matter the time of year, when walking in these hills be prepared and equipped for all weather conditions. On their website, the Met Office have a specific mountain weather forecast for the Yorkshire Dales. This can be accessed at
http://www.metoffice.gov.uk/loutdoor/mountainsafety

5. The Maps

Just the one map is required to cover the walks in this book, Ordinance Survey Explorer OL30 Yorkshire Dales North and Central, which covers the bulk of the dale.

The route descriptions included in this book are meant as a guide and although under normal conditions they should be sufficient to guide you round the route they are not intended to replace the use of the relevant map. This countryside can be wild and rough, which is part of it's attraction, and the weather can be very changeable. It is quite possible to set off in brilliant sunshine and then to find that later, low cloud and rain has come rolling in and visibility is very poor. The ability to navigate with map and compass is a required skill to safely traverse these hills and it would be extremely foolhardy to venture out with just this guidebook and no map.

6. Accommodation, Facilities and Attractions

Set around a large sloping green which is split by the B6270 road, Reeth is a delightful and popular location for the visitor. With the country's most popular long distance walk, Wainwright's Coast to Coast, passing through the village it is also very familiar with and catering for the needs of the visiting walker.

For a small location, there is an abundance of cafes, pubs and shops including a post office, general stores, newsagent, bakery, garage and craft shops. From personal experience I can also highly recommend the ice cream parlour, despite numerous visits I'm still working my way through their full list of flavours.

Set at various locations around the green lie the three pubs of the village, the Buck Hotel, the Kings Arms and the Black Bull with it's now semi-famous upside down sign that has resulted from a long running planning dispute with the National Park Authority. There are many bed and breakfast establishments, guest houses and holiday homes within the village plus the Burgoyne Hotel, the visitor can be a little bit spoilt for choice. For those who's tastes are slightly different there are also a number of camping and caravan sites both in and around the village. Contacting the National Park Information Centre or Reeth's own website, see the section below for details of both, can help you choose the most appropriate one.

Tucked away in the old Methodist Day School, built in 1836, is the Swaledale Museum. Following the signs from the green will lead you to it's hidden location down a small, narrow side street. For those interested in the history of the dale or even just general history, it can provide a fascinating diversion for a couple of hours. For more information and opening hours visit the website at **www. swaledalemuseum.org/**

Located in Bagshaws Yard, just round the corner from the YDNPA Visitor Centre at Hudson House, is Swaledale Outdoors the only outdoor shop in the upper dale above Richmond. A modern conversion of an old yard, the shop stocks the best in outdoor clothing and equipment for both the walker and runner and even

if not purchasing any gear it is well worth the visit just for a browse and the expert local knowledge of the area that the owner, Richard, has. Future developments include a 'map room and refuge' area where you can flick through books and maps on the dale while planning your walk over a cup of coffee or tea or just recounting your experiences of the day while you recover from your exertions. There are even plans for wi-fi connections and an overnight boot servicing facility. Their website can be found at **www.swaledaleoutdoors.co.uk**

During June, Reeth acts as the focus for hundreds of outdoor enthusiasts, both walkers and runners, as it stages the annual 23 mile Swaledale Marathon. This event is one of the most popular long distance challenges in the north of England and is normally full within weeks of the entry lists being opened. Hosted by the Swaledale Outdoor Club since 1979, further details can be found on their website at **www.swaledaleoutdoorclub.org.uk**

In the months of May and June, Reeth becomes the centre of the internationally acclaimed Swaledale Festival, a two week celebration of music that is performed at many locations throughout the dale. The festival also features a number of guided walks.

As with many farming communities in the north of England, Reeth has it's own agricultural show, Reeth Show, which is held in the fields between Reeth and Fremington on the final Wednesday in August each year. While in late September and early October, the Richmond Walking and Book Festival is held. Although based further down the dale at Richmond, this week long celebration of walking features many walks in the upper dale surrounding Reeth.

7. Tourist Information Centres & Websites

Within Swaledale there are two Tourist Information Centres, one operated by Richmondshire District Council and situated in Richmond, the other operated by the Yorkshire Dales National Park and located within Reeth itself. Contact details of both are below.

Richmond Tourist Information Centre
Friary Gardens
Victoria Road
Richmond
North Yorkshire DL10 4AJ
Tel. 01748 850252

Yorkshire Dales National Park Tourist Information
Hudson House

The Green
Reeth
Richmond
North Yorkshire DL11 6TB
Tel. 01748 884059

In addition to the TIC's the Yorkshire Dales National Park Authority operate a very useful website giving information on the flora, fauna, geology, attractions and events in the Yorkshire Dales National Park. The website can be found at **www.yorkshiredales.org.uk/**

As with many small places nowadays, the community of Reeth has it's own website. This has details on the attractions of the village, it's people and history and other relevant information such as accommodation and events/what's going on and covers the area surrounding the village plus the tributary valley of Arkengarthdale. It is an excellent site and for the visitor it is well worth a look and can be found at **www.reeth.org/**

8. Lead Mining Glossary

A few of the terms used in the text of the book may be unfamiliar to those not used to the lead mining industry and so a brief glossary is listed below to help you better understand some of the features that you will encounter on the walks.

Dressing floor
An area where the lead ore would be crushed and processed to remove the waste prior to going to the smelt mill. During this process, or dressing as it was known, the ore would be crushed and ground up until it was the consistency of sand with the final product produced from this process being know as lead concentrate. The dressing floor would usually be close to the mine entrance so that there would be no costly transporting of waste material, only the valuable lead concentrate would be moved to the smelt mill.

Hush
A rather environmentally unfriendly method of extracting ore from the ground. A dam would be erected at the top of a slope and a head of water built up, this would then be released in a torrent to flow down the slope scouring off the top soil and other loose rock exposing the vein of lead, the vein would then be worked with hammer and pick. Hushes were often used in the exploratory stage to determine both where the vein was and in which direction it ran. In most cases the hush didn't tend to go deep into the vein and so they were then often followed by driving a level at the bottom of the hush to access the lower levels

of ore.

Flue

The chimney from a smelt mill. They often ran a considerable distance up the side of a hill before terminating in a chimney on the hill top. Built to remove the toxic fumes from the smelting process they also provided a secondary purpose in creating a draught for the furnaces helping to increase their operating temperature.

Leat

A man-made water channel built to carry a flow of water to a specific location.

Level

A horizontal tunnel dug into the side of the hill to access the vein, also known as an adit. Normally located at the bottom of the hill they would usually be constructed with a slight upward angle to allow water from the mine to drain out. Drainage was a secondary purpose of a level and is why many of them have a small stream running out of them. Often levels and shafts connect underground to form a complex of tunnels.

Shaft

A vertical tunnel dug straight down into the vein. Normally located on the top of a hill, shafts are distinguished by a round ring or "donut" of spoil that circled the opening of the shaft. Shafts could be deep or shallow with the deeper ones often connecting to levels. Shallower shafts would only be around 30 metres deep with a number of them forming a straight line across the moor as they follow the line of the vein. Shallow shafts are also known as bell pits.

Smelt mill

A building where the lead was extracted by heating the lead concentrate in a furnace until the molten lead would separate from the rock.

Spoil

The waste material from the mining process that is discarded around the mine and processing sites. Nowadays all waste is just generally called spoil although during the days of mining there were specific names for waste from different parts of the process such as "deads" for non-ore bearing rock and stone extracted from the mine.

One of the two chimneys still standing at Hurst.

WALK 1: HURST

The lead mines surrounding the hamlet of Hurst were, at their peak, some of the most profitable in Swaledale and many miners from Reeth made the daily trek up and over Fremington Edge before starting a hard six hour shift underground. At the end of the shift, then they had the long walk back. No matter the time of year or the weather, lines of miners crossed the moor. If you couldn't make it to work then you couldn't earn and wages meant food for both you and your dependants. Starvation and hardship were never far away for a miner and his family.

This route retraces the miner's footsteps along the old track between Reeth and Hurst crossing as it goes the stark remnants of the mining grounds. From Hurst you then follow another old miner's track over to Arkengarthdale, again, from where many miners made the daily slog to work.

DISTANCE: 7.5 miles (12 km)
ASCENT: 1.332 feet (406 metres)

TERRAIN: The first half of the walk follows moorland tracks up and over Fremington Edge to Hurst and then back to Storthwaite Hall in Arkengarthdale. From there field paths are followed back to Reeth. One section of field path does cross a rather boggy area of ground near the Arkle Beck. The climb up Fremington Edge is long and, in places, fairly steep. The descent down and through the Fell End quarries to Storthwaite Hall is also quite steep.

TIME: 3½ to 4 ½ hours.

START: Reeth Village Green. GR SE 038 992.

DOGS: The walk is all on public rights of way and so dogs are allowed. However, please keep them under close control especially when going over the moors of Fremington Edge during the nesting season of May and June. At this time, even though rights of way are not affected, the moors normally have their open access temporally suspended. Livestock will be encountered throughout this walk.

ACCESS: This walk is all on public rights of way.

Grid References :

Reeth village green	038 992
Fremington Edge	044 007
Track/road junction	046 023
Gate	031 022
Storthwaite Hall	018 022
Castle Farm House	030 009
Track/path junction	041 001
Path/road junction	042 992
Reeth village green	038 992

FGS Grading

Grading is F6 [D1, N1, T1, R1, H2]

Distance	1	6 – 12 miles
Navigation	1	Basic navigation skills needed
Terrain	1	50 – 75% on graded track or path 25 – 50% off track
Remoteness	1	Countryside in fairly close proximity to habitation – at least 80% of the route within 2 miles
Height	2	Over 125 ft per mile

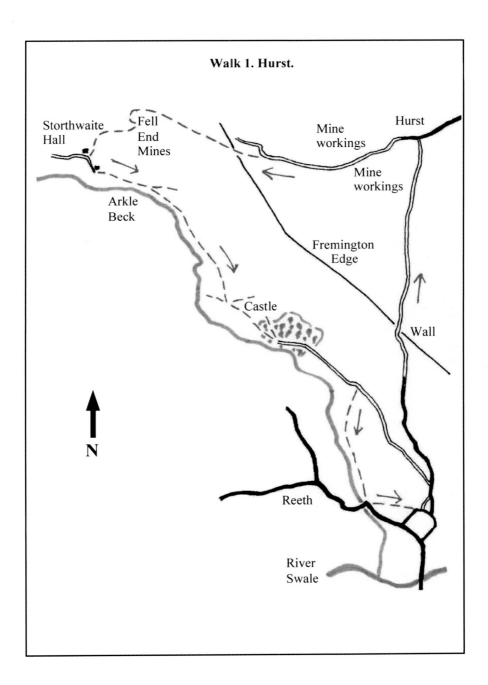

Walk 1. Hurst.

Storthwaite Hall

Fell End Mines

Mine workings

Hurst

Mine workings

Arkle Beck

Fremington Edge

Castle

Wall

N

Reeth

River Swale

THE WALK

1. From Reeth village green head back down the B6270 road towards Richmond. Leave the village and cross the bridge over the Arkle Beck. As you do so Durant car sales is immediately on the corner and just after that, on the left hand side of the road, is a footpath sign pointing through a small wooden gate in the wall. Go through the gate but instead of going in the direction indicated by the signpost bear to the right where there is another signpost and gate in the wall on that side. See the photo below.

The path through the fields is well-trodden and is relatively easy to follow as it heads in the 11 o'clock position to a wall with another wooden gate and footpath signpost. Go through and turn right to follow the wall on the right passing through another two walls that lie in front, the first by a wooden gate and the second by a gap. The path then joins a farm track leading to a gate which itself leads onto a narrow tarmac road.

You come out onto the road just in front of Brambles cottage which is on the left side. Turn left immediately after the cottage to follow a stony track that runs uphill alongside the building and after a short climb comes out onto a tarmac lane which is the access road for the White House perched half-way up Fremington Edge. Turn left and follow the road as it climbs uphill under a canopy of trees before coming to a gate leading onto the open side of the hill. The tarmac continues on until it abruptly changes into two stony tracks, one bearing left to the White House and the other climbing steeply uphill. Yes, you've guessed it, you continue going steeply uphill to follow this track all the way to the top of Fremington. As it climbs the track passes through and beside some old chert quarries.

Chert is a hard stone very much like flint and in prehistoric times was used for tool making in those areas where flint was not readily available. When you see the sharp edges on some of the broken stones you'll understand why. In more modern times both the black and white forms of chert were quarried and the stone itself was ground into a fine powder which was then used in the production of fine china and pottery. A number of old chert quarries are passed on this walk.

Towards the top the track does split into two but it doesn't matter which one you take as they both join up again in front of the gate leading onto the open moor. **GR 044 007.**

2. Go through the gate and continue to follow the track across Marrick Moor. This area was quite heavily mined for lead and this has left quite a lot of industrial dereliction which can be seen as you get closer to Hurst including the remains of two chimneys. The track terminates on the tarmac road that provides access to Hurst, **GR 046 023**.

Descending to Hurst.

Despite all the villages and hamlets in Upper Swaledale having links to lead mining, Hurst is the only one that is built-up close to the mines, rather like a colliery village. The hamlet is situated on the moors at a height of 1,200 feet. Lead mining in the vicinity is known to go back to Roman times and the village's existence is a direct result of the expansion of mining in the 17th century. Although it is difficult to believe now but at it's peak Hurst consisted of sixty-six dwellings and three inns. However, living at Hurst was not the most pleasant of locations. The single-storey thatched dwellings were recognised in 1841 as being some of the worst housing in Swaledale. In 1885 the mines of Hurst were producing 800 tons of lead per year but by 1890 the market had collapsed, mining had become uneconomic and all activity in the area had ceased. With the end of employment the village began to empty of people. Now Hurst is little more than a hamlet surrounded by old spoil heaps, abandoned levels and the two ruined chimneys from the steam engines that powered the Cat and Brown shafts.

3. Turn left to follow the road for a short distance to a gate, where you go through to follow the track on the other side. This makes it's way through a landscape of spoil heaps and disused pits and shafts. Eventually this does give way to moor and the track does finally approach a stone wall and here leave it to follow a short path over to a gate in this wall. **GR 031 022**.

Approaching the wall and gate.

4. Go through the gate and as it starts to descend the path is relatively easy to follow. After a short while you start entering an area of old mine workings and here the path starts to be lined by a series of small cairns, some of which have wooden posts with yellow way markers on, these are easy to follow from one to another. The path takes a sharp turn to the left and starts to descend quite steeply down through a quarry face that is the Fell End Mines.

Descending through the Fell End Mines.

Although steep and stony it is not a particularly difficult descent and once through the stones and tips, it approaches the walls above the valley's field system where it meets a gate and a wooden sign post pointing out the way 'to Langthwaite'. Go through the gate and follow the path down as it changes into a sunken track and eventually becomes a walled lane which emerges at a gate alongside Storthwaite Hall. A grandly named farm house. **GR 018 022.**

5. Go through the gate and turn left to continue along the walled lane until you come to a gate alongside a very nice farmhouse. Pass through the gate and follow the obvious path across the sheep field and through the next wall. As you approach the other side of the field, the sound of running water tells you that you are close to the Arkle Beck and here you'll find a footbridge hidden in the trees. Ignore the bridge and stay on the left bank to go through the gate in front. Here you'll find a marker post indicating a bridleway heading away to the left and a footpath bearing right to follow the beck. Stay on the footpath to continue following the water. The path is easy to follow as it stays close to the beck. Eventually you'll come to a marker post which directs you on a path through the reed beds at the side of the beck. In the past, duckboard bridges have been erected here to keep you out of the worst but these are often swept away when the beck floods. If there are no duckboards, then stick to the bank of the beck until you come to a wire fence. At this point the fence has been beaten down and you can cross it but the ground on the other side is very boggy and you would be better off following the fence a little bit further up to the trees where there is a gap and the ground is a bit drier. Go through the gap and cross some duckboards to come to the first in a series of marker posts.

Heading through the reed beds.

These guide you straight on while the Arkle Beck bends away to the right in a long loop. As you follow the posts, with the occasional dollop of yellow paint on stones and walls to help, the buildings of Castle Farm appear on the left but stay with the posts to head for Castle Farm House which lies straight ahead of you. As you walk across the last field in front of the house, head to the left side of the building to find a footpath marker. **GR 030 009.**

4. At the side of the house continue on round the left of the buildings and through the gap between the barn and the wall, then head for a splodge of yellow paint on a stone at the top of the ruined wall ahead of you. The path itself goes over this wall to enter the next field. The ruined walls here are much older than the buildings of Castle Farm House and, although ruined, have a more substantial appearance to them. Linking the 'Castle' name with the walls and the fact that some of them appear to have structures built into them suggests that in past years this must have been a sizable settlement with protective walls.

The walls of Castles.

Cross straight over to the waymarked gated stile opposite and then follow the path as it descends across four fields passing both woods and a ruined farm cottage on the left. At the end of the fourth field, when you are once again close to the Arkle Beck, enter the wood to come to a three-way signpost. Ignore the unmarked path by the side of the beck and instead follow the track that heads uphill away from the stream and which is shown as a bridleway. Follow the track through the wood passing evidence of quarrying hidden in the undergrowth and the remains of a disused lime kiln, this was very probably the recipient of the material extracted from the quarries. A couple of fields after you have exited the woods the track comes to a large three-way signpost on the right with a gate and stile in the wall. **GR 041 001.**

5. Leave the track to cross the stile and head down towards the Arkle Beck which can be seen below. The path goes to the right of the barn in front and through a series of fields following the waymarkers, the blobs of yellow paint and the white hand-painted arrows. When you do get to the valley floor, and after passing to the left of a small barn, you will arrive at two gates directly in front of you. Go through the left-hand gate and follow the right side of the wall past a farm and after a short distance you'll come to a stile on the right that exits out onto the roadside. **GR 042 992.**

6. Cross the stile onto the road and turn right to head over the road bridge and follow the road up into Reeth

The western most dyke and ditch with the wall running along the top of the dyke.

WALK 2: THE SOUTHERN DYKES

A shorter walk this but a nice winter one when a light dusting of snow can really highlight the land forms and show off some of the landscape archaeology that exists in this part of the dale. The two main features of this walk are a couple of the Dark Age defensive dykes erected across the width of the valley to protect the native Celtic kingdom of the Swale from the encroaching Anglian invaders.

The Anglians were a Germanic people who first started invading and settling in the northern part of this country during the years following the departure of the

Romans. It is from these people and the other related Germanic tribes, the Saxons who settled in the south, that the Anglo-Saxon kingdom of England, Angleland, developed.

DISTANCE: 3.6 miles (5.7 km)

ASCENT: 397 feet (121 metres)

TERRAIN: Most of the route is on field path although there is a short section following a path across the open moor and two very short road sections. The route has only the one real climb in it, when it goes up through the fields on the side of the valley to reach the open moor and a short, steep descent as you come down from Bleak House to the riverbank.

TIME: 2½ to 3½ hours.

START: Reeth Village Green. GR SE 038 992

DOGS: The route is all on rights of way and so dogs are permitted. However, livestock will be encountered throughout the walk and, in particular, a couple of the fields that are passed through are used for lambing so dogs do need to be kept on a lead at all times. Some of the stiles encountered are set high in the walls and are also quite narrow, in all probability you will need to lift your dog over these and if it is a big dog then you may be struggling.

ACCESS: The route is all on public rights of way.

Grid References :

Reeth village green	038 992
Swing bridge	032 989
Track/road junction	042 985
Gate	044 979
Stile	040 979
Track/road junction	036 982
Reeth village green	038 992

FGS Grading
Grading is F4 [D0, N1, T1, R1, H1]

Distance	0	Up to 6 miles
Navigation	1	Basic navigation skills needed
Terrain	1	50 – 75% on graded track or path 25 – 50% off track
Remoteness	1	Countryside in fairly close proximity to habitation – at least 80% of the route within 2 miles
Height	1	Over 100 ft per mile

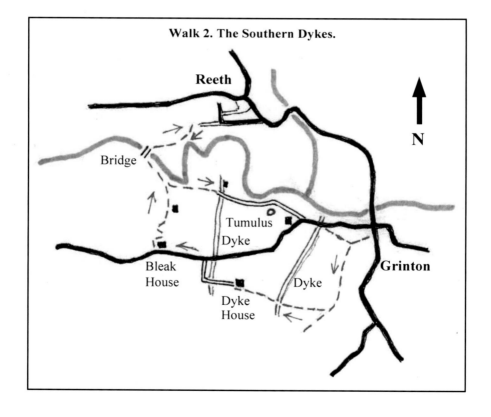

Walk 2. The Southern Dykes.

THE WALK

1. From the village green head past The Black Bull pub and Tourist Information Centre into Anvil Square and follow it as it bears to the right. Here look up for a sign that is placed high up on the wall of the pottery on the left and states "to the river" and follow the direction indicated down a little narrow lane. At the end of the lane, go straight on for a short distance to the road in front where you turn left to go down to a T-junction and here turn right to follow the road past the doctor's surgery. When the tarmac ends and the lane becomes unsurfaced, continue on to the end where you come to a footpath sign pointing both straight on and also down a lane on the left. Turn left and descend down the lane, through the gate at the bottom and then follow the well trodden path that bears to the right through a couple of meadows to come to Reeth Swing Bridge. **GR 032 989**.

A snowy Harkerside seen from the outward lane.

2. Cross the swing bridge and once on the other side turn left as shown by the sign 'Grinton' and follow the riverbank downstream. Note that the riverbanks here don't normally look as they are shown on the OS map. The Swale is a very fast flowing river and prone to violent flooding, meaning that it frequently alters it's course as it flows through these low lying meadows. Follow the riverbank round until you come to two large wooden gateposts which mark the start of an old lane. Go between them towards a gate and enter the next field. Here follow the left hand edge of the field to come to another gate this time leading into a walled lane. Follow the lane as it heads up over a low hill and as you descend down the other side you'll pass a field on the left with a building in it. Here stop and turn around to view the remains of the first dyke encountered on the walk as it runs on both sides of the lane..

The line of the dyke heading down from the lane towards the river.

Continue following the lane and after 200 metres you'll come to a stretch where it runs next to the river with a low wall between you and the water. At the end of this section the lane rises as it leaves the river and here, in a field on the right the distinctive shape of a burial mound, shown as a tumulus on the map, can be seen. Keep following the lane until it joins a tarmac road. **GR 042 985.**

The burial mound silhouetted against the sky.

3. Bear left to join the road and after approximately 150 metres, the bottom end of the second dyke can be seen running down the hill on the right towards the road. Continue along the road for another 20/30 metres to come to a footpath sign and a stile on the right hand side. Leave the road to cross the stile and head for a second stile a few metres up the wall on the left. Cross this stile and then make for the wide gap in the wall opposite and from here you'll see another stile

The line of the second dyke running up the hill.

facing you in the wall on the other side of the field. Make for that but when you get there don't cross it, instead turn right and, keeping the small stream on your left, head uphill to find yet another stile at the top of the field. Cross this stile and go straight ahead making for the little gate on the left side of the barn. When you get to the barn take the opportunity of turning round and looking at the view. Well worth it. Go through the gate and go straight ahead to join a grass track and continue following it up the hill to come to a gate. **GR 044 979**.

4. Go through the gate and immediately turn to the right to follow a faint path that goes past two wooden structures that look as it they may be part of a clay pigeon shooting apparatus. As you get further along, the path gets more pronounced and climbs slightly as it runs across the side of the hill above but parallel to the wall below. After a short while you'll approach a wall in front that runs all the way down to the valley. When you get to this wall you'll need to turn right to follow it the short distance down the bank to the wall corner and a gated stile. **GR 040 979**.

At this point the remains of the second dyke, encountered while walking along the road in the valley floor, are clearly visible on the right. The wall on that side is built along the top of the dyke and runs all the way down to the valley.

5. Go over the stile and head straight across the field following the wall on the right to come to another stile in the wall corner. Clamber over the stile and continue straight ahead past the aptly named Dyke House to another stile next to a barn, this one being set even higher in the wall than the last. Once over, head to the track on the right and follow it to a wall corner where it turns to the right and descends. However, before continuing round the wall corner, look over the other side of the wall to see the unmistakeable outline of a dyke and ditch. This is the top end of the first dyke that was encountered while walking along the walled lane down on the valley floor. The dyke does continue on uphill from the wall corner but the remains of this aren't so prominent as the section heading down to the river. Follow the track round the fence corner and descend down to the road. **GR 036 982**.

The second dyke and ditch running down to the valley.

6. Turn left onto the road and follow it for 350 metres to come to a cattle grid. Cross the grid and there is a house on the right, Bleak House, on the left side of which is a gate which gives access to a grass track that curves down to a barn on the slopes below. To the right of the barn is a red metal gate, go through and walk to the left, round the building and look for a stile in the wall on the right

Bleak House.

Looking down on to the swing bridge and Reeth from Bleak House.

about half-way down the field. Once through this, head for a gated stile to the left of the building over on your left. Go through the second gate immediately opposite and once in the next field head downhill towards the left corner but making for the right of a small barn where you will find a stile just in front of a small tree. Turn left and follow the riverbank back to the visible swing bridge. Cross and bear right to retrace your steps along the path and lane leading back to the village. Once at the junction turn left to head through the houses and then take the first turning right to go up the narrow lane back to the village green.

The Long Scar dyke and ditch looking down towards Reeth.

The Celtic warrior stands at his lonely vigil atop the stone ramparts that stretch across the dale. As the wind blows against his mail shirt and leather armour he peers into the early morning light. His eyes open for any incursion from the fierce Anglian invaders, intent on driving both him and his people out of their own land.

THE GRINTON - FREMINGTON DYKES

Unnoticed by many, stretching across the dale are two great earthworks called the Grinton - Fremington Dykes. For many years it was thought that these were prehistoric constructions, possibly made during the Iron Age. However, recent research, in particular by the landscape archaeologist Andrew Fleming, has shown that these dykes were actually built during the so-called 'Dark Ages'. That turbulent period after the Romans left and during which it is thought that there was a revival in the native British Celtic culture before the coming of the Anglians and the Saxons.

The dykes are now thought to have been built at some point during the fifth, sixth and even the early seventh century. Their purpose being to mark the boundary between the native British people and the advancing Anglians who are known to have had a kingdom further east centred on Catraeth, thought to be modern-day Catterick.

Sitting just west of Grinton, the two dykes lie about 500 metres apart, each of them comprised of a massive bank and ditch. Both of the dykes can be traced,

The line of the western-most dyke running across the southern side of the valley with Reeth in the background.

One of the northern dykes running through the village of Fremington.

although at times with some difficulty, down to the flood-plain of the river and again rising on the northern side up to the bottom of Fremington Edge. Further south, running across Harkerside, is a continuation of the dykes, this one being called Long Scar and which is encountered on Walk 9. Further east lies a third dyke, lying on the valley floor just across the river from Marrick Abbey.

The positioning of the dykes indicates that they were a defence for both Upper Swaledale and Arkengarthdale from invaders from the east. Each dyke is comprised of a high, broad bank with a deep ditch on the eastern side, the side from which intruders would be expected to come. On the western-most dyke a break across it, close to where the enclosed track passes over it, also shows that the bank had a carefully built stone face on it's eastern side, presumably to make it harder to scale. It is not known whether the dyke was topped with some sort of wooden palisade or other kind of barrier maybe even a stone rampart. No excavation work has been done on these earthworks and so their original structure can only be imagined. However, excavations on similar monuments throughout the country have revealed ditches up to four metres (15 ft) deep with ramparts up to three to four metres (9 - 15 ft) high built topping the dyke.

During this period banked dykes and ditches were a commonly used method of earthwork defences. There are other examples at the head of Coverdale, one of the side dales of Wensleydale, Tor Dyke, thought to be the northern boundary of the Celtic kingdom of Craven and further east in Swaledale, just the other side of Richmond, can be seen a few remains of Scots Dyke, an earthwork running roughly from north to south for a distance of several miles. However, the most well-known is Offa's Dyke on the borders of Wales and England.

Marrick Abbey seen from the path up to Steps Wood.

WALK 3: MARRICK ABBEY & FREMINGTON EDGE

Swaledale has a long history of human habitation going back over thousands of years and on this walk you'll encounter fragments of this rich tapestry and see how, even now, the landscape is still shaped by humans who are long gone. From the lead mining of the 18th and 19th centuries to the Medieval religious houses, going further back to the Dark Ages after the Romans left, the Celtic Iron Age and beyond to the days of the Bronze Age when humans were just starting to build permanent settlements in these upland areas, this is one of those walks that makes you see the landscape with new eyes.

DISTANCE: 7.3 miles (11.7 km)

ASCENT: 935 feet (285 metres)

TERRAIN: This route is mainly on field paths and moorland tracks although there are a couple of lengthy road sections on quiet country lanes. The ascent of Fremington Edge is from the side and so is long and gradual although the descent down the front is a good bit steeper.

TIME: 3½ to 4½ hours.

START: Reeth Village Green. GR SE 038 992

DOGS: The walk is all on public rights of way and so dogs are allowed. However, please keep them under close control especially when going over the moors of Fremington Edge during the nesting season of May to June. At this time, even though rights of way are not affected, the moors normally have their open access temporally suspended. There is two sections of road walking on quiet country lanes where you may meet vehicles.

ACCESS: This walk is all on public rights of way.

Grid References :

Reeth village green	038 992
Grinton Bridge	046 986
Marrick Abbey	067 978
Lane junction	076 981
Road T-junction	067 991
Cairn	051 000
Gate & stile	044 007
Reeth village green	038 992

FGS Grading

Grading is F5 [D1, N1, T0, R1, H2]

Distance	1	6 – 12 miles
Navigation	1	Basic navigation skills needed
Terrain	0	75% + on graded track or path
Remoteness	1	Countryside in fairly close proximity to habitation – at least 80% of the route within 2 miles
Height	2	Over 125 ft per mile

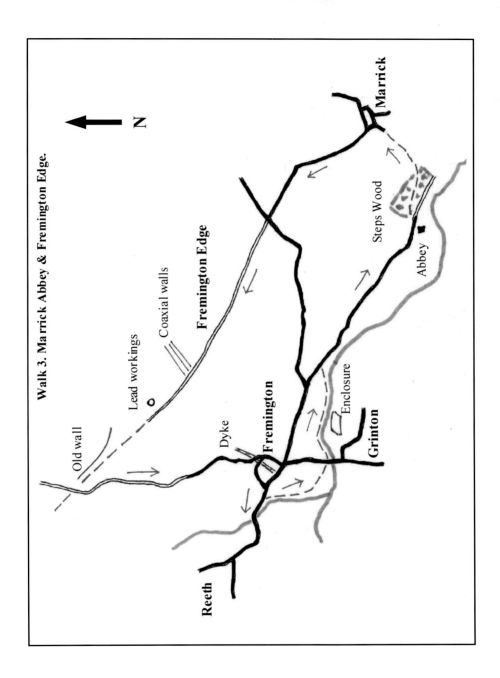

Walk 3. Marrick Abbey & Fremington Edge.

N

Old wall

Lead workings

Coaxial walls

Fremington Edge

Dyke

Fremington

Enclosure

Grinton

Marrick

Steps Wood

Abbey

Reeth

THE WALK

1. From the green follow the road back towards Richmond and cross the road bridge over the Arkle Beck, follow the pavement on the right side of the road and two hundred metres after the bridge leave the roadside to turn right through a small gate that has a footpath signpost next to it. See photo right. Follow the path alongside the beck and then, after the farm, when it turns away from the beck, through the fields to exit out onto the road next to Grinton Bridge. **GR 046 986.**

2. Cross the road and slightly to the left is a parking space that sits at the head of a track that goes down to the river. Follow this track down to the river and then bear left to follow the riverside path downstream. Through the trees that line the riverbank the houses of Grinton can be seen on the other side of the river, once the houses have been passed two large mounds can be seen on the opposite bank. The second mound, which is a glacial moraine, is the site of a fortified Iron Age settlement. Unfortunately the tree cover prevents a good view but later on in the walk a clearer opportunity presents itself. After a short while the path enters an open field that borders the River Swale before a little climb to exit out onto the side of a tarmac lane. Turn right to follow the lane to Marrick Abbey. **GR 067 978.**

The ancient priory of Marrick was founded for the Benedictine nuns around the year 1150. It was established by Roger De Aske who gave it land, grazing rights and other property including the Church of St Andrew in Marrick. Life at the priory seems to have been more relaxed than the more severe lifestyle normally associated with nuns. The rich grazing rights allowed flocks of sheep to be kept giving a valuable income from the sale of wool, this meant that the nuns could employ as many secular woman as required for work regarded as unbecoming for the nuns to perform themselves. At the time of the dissolution of the monasteries, Marrick Priory was given the distinction of being allowed to exist for several more years and was not finally surrendered to the crown till November 1540. By the time of the surrender there remained a prioress and sixteen nuns at the priory.

3. After the Abbey, cross the cattle grid and then leave the tarmac to cross the stile on the left next to the signpost "Marrick 1/3". Follow the green path that

365 Stone steps from the priory to the village of Marrick and the church of St Andrew. This was the line between the two that was used by both the nuns and the villages to travel to work and practice their faith. Now many of the steps have disappeared or collapsed leaving just this stone trod climbing through Steps Wood.

heads uphill to enter Steps Wood. Once inside the paved path is obvious to follow as it climbs up through the wood.

When you exit continue following the wall on the right which leads to two small buildings at the end of the field. Once there, go though the gate and, ignoring the footpath on the right, continue straight ahead past the old Wesleyan Chapel and St Andrew's Church to join a tarmac lane leading into Marrick. After a short distance the lane comes to a junction with another lane on the left, next to Harland House. **GR 076 981**.

The hamlet that we now call Marrick once went by the name Hellingsley which comes from the Old English for 'Helen's clearing'. This refers back to when the dale was completely wooded and the existence of St Ellen's Well to the east of the hamlet. The name Marrick probably applied to the riverside where the priory was sited.

4. Turn left and a hundred metres later turn left again to follow the lane for 15/20 minutes walking as it slowly climbs uphill to eventually come to a T-Junction. **GR 067 991**.

Up until the 1830's the road in front was the main road from Richmond into the upper reaches of Swaledale. This centuries old route was replaced by a newly-constructed turnpike road down on the valley floor which still serves as the main road.

5. Go over the road in front to cross a stile which is slightly to the left and marked by a footpath sign. Follow the track as it climbs next to the right-hand wall, passing a newly restored lime kiln, and comes to a very dilapidated gate that at the time of test walking was on the verge of collapse. Go through or under and then follow the wall on the left to a second, more substantial gate onto the open moor. Continue following the path next to the wall on the left and after a short distance this changes to become a more substantial track. Stay on the track as it slowly climbs the edge of the moor.

As you climb, look over the wall on the left for some excellent views over the other side of the valley. Look down into the valley floor and the village of Grinton lies beneath you. From Grinton let your eyes wander slightly downstream and the two mounds that you were trying to see through the trees while you were walking next to the river can be clearly seen. On the second, larger mound, is the square impression of the Iron Age settlement. What couldn't be seen earlier is clearly laid out below you now.

Looking down onto the ramparts of the Iron Age defended settlement at Grinton.

Continue on the track and just before you reach the summit there is a subtle change in the nature of the stones that comprise the surface of the track.

In a couple of places there are larger stones going left to right across the track. These are the remains of Bronze Age coaxial field walls that date back over four thousand years. Swaledale is one of the major locations in this country, second only to Dartmoor, for the existence of these walls. In this case, the walls start above Fremington Edge and head off over Marrick Moor to build what was once a very extensive field system that may have extended as far as Shaw Beck. The track has obviously been built over the remains of the wall but evidence does exist in the heather to

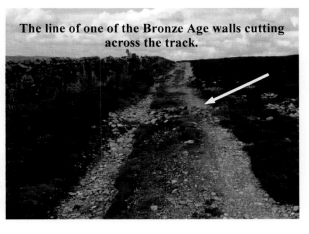

The line of one of the Bronze Age walls cutting across the track.

show the walls continuing on across the moor. For more detail on coaxial walls see page 64.

39

Stay on the track as it goes over the top of the moor and after a short distance an area of old spoil heaps and workings is reached. Here you'll find a large cairn by the side of the track. (**GR 051 000**).

This part of the moor was extensively worked for lead, the result of which has left these large donut shaped mounds of spoil that surrounded the old shafts. The shafts normally follow a straight line as they follow the line of the vein over the moor. From the cairn, the line of the shafts can be seen on both sides of the wall.

The old shafts and spoil heaps along the top of Fremington Edge.

Continue following the wall to come to a cross-wall with a large ladder stile going over it. The top of the stile gives an excellent view up the length of Swaledale. The rusty pile of metal on the other side of the wall is all that remains of a radio transmitter. Once over the stile continue following the path next to the left hand wall. As you walk, look to the right to see a raised earthen line running across the moor, this is an old medieval field wall dating back several centuries. You'll soon come to a second cross-wall, this time with a stile and a gate in it. **GR 044 007**.

6. Go through the gate to the track behind it and then turn left to go through the gate there and emerge on the top of Fremington Edge high above Reeth. Follow the track as it bends to the left and descends down the Edge. When the track passes the access track to the White House it becomes tarmac and then passes through a gate to become a walled lane and more of a road. After a while the land on the left of the road becomes a bit more wooded.

As you emerge from under the trees the field on the left side of the road is worthy of a look. Look closely and you'll see a small ridge that starts on the left side of the field and as it moves across slowly grows larger. This is the Fremington Dyke, one of the series of earthworks that date back to the Dark Ages, see the feature on the Grinton - Fremington Dykes. At this point the dyke is not so prominent but presumably went across the field to butt up against the slope of Fremington Edge at some point above you on the left. To the right the dyke runs in a straight line down the slope to the valley floor and across towards the river. As you follow the road, it bends sharply to the left and cuts through the dyke and here you can see a cross section of it and get an impression of how tall it must have been when still pristine.

The road itself follows the dyke down and when you enter High Fremington you'll come to a junction where if you follow the road on the right, it will once again cut through the dyke before descending down to the main road. If you so wish, when you get to the road you can turn left for a short distance and from the right side of the road you get a good view of the dyke as it comes down to the road behind Draycott Hall before turning round and following the main road back into Reeth.

Fremington Dyke behind Draycott Hall.

Built in the 1700's as the home to the mine-owning Denys family, Draycott Hall is a very visible sign of the wealth that lead mining produced. At least for the mine owners !!

It is thought that Fremington originated as an Anglian settlement somewhere between 750 and 950 AD. It's positioning on either side of one of the dykes suggests that this was after the dyke had fallen into disuse, possibly when the influence in the dale was no longer native Celtic but had been replaced by Anglian newcomers. The name Fremington is thought to come from the personal name 'Frema' - Frema's farm.

41

Walking along the ramparts of Maiden Castle.

WALK 4: MAIDEN CASTLE

DISTANCE: 4.8 miles (7.6 km)

ASCENT: 656 feet (200 metres)

TERRAIN: Mainly field and moorland paths. In the height of summer the moorland paths may be overgrown by heather but they should still be relatively easy to follow. There are a couple of short, steep climbs leading from the riverside up to Maiden Castle.

TIME: 3 to 4 hours

START: Reeth Village Green. GR SE038 992

DOGS: This walk is entirely on rights of way so dogs are allowed under close control. Livestock can be found throughout the entire route and at one point you do walk through a farmyard complete with barking border collie. There are a couple of short stretches of road walking plus the start and finishing sections going in and out of Reeth are also on road.

ACCESS: This route follows public rights of way throughout.

Grid References :

Reeth village green	038 992
Swing bridge	032 989
Path/road junction	019 983
Maiden Castle	021 981
Path junction	025 980
Gate	031 981
Gate	039 977
Track/road junction	046 981
Reeth village green	038 992

FGS Grading

Grading is F5 [D0, N1, T1, R1, H2]

Distance	**0**	Up to 6 miles
Navigation	**1**	Basic navigation skills needed
Terrain	**1**	50 – 75% on graded track or path 25 – 50% off track
Remoteness	**1**	Countryside in fairly close proximity to habitation – at least 80% of the route within 2 miles
Height	**2**	Over 125 ft per mile

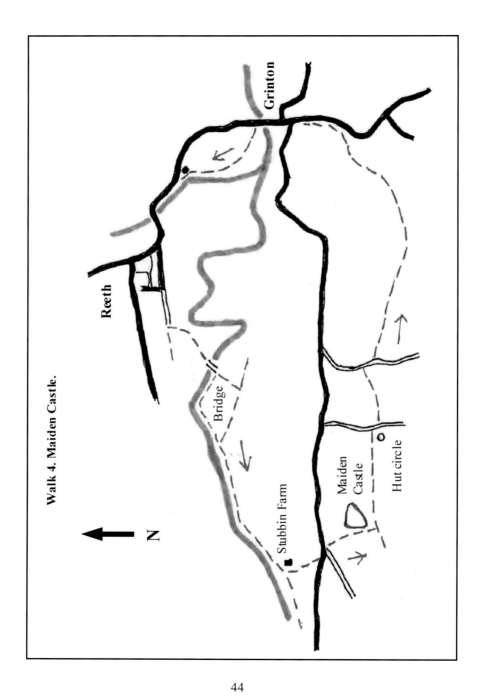

Walk 4. Maiden Castle.

N

Grinton

Reeth

Bridge

Stubbin Farm

Maiden Castle

Hut circle

THE WALK

1. From the village green head past the King's Arms and Black Bull pubs to come to the small green at Anvil Square. See photo above. Pass the green and following the sign 'to the river' which is high up the wall of The Garden House, go down a small lane between the walls. As the lane emerges from the walls onto a narrow road, go straight on to come to a street where you turn left to follow it for a short distance to a T-junction. Turn right to follow the signs 'Swing Bridge' and 'Doctors Surgery' and head down the narrow lane passing the surgery on the way. At the last house, Quakers Garth, the tarmac ends and the surface becomes unmetaled. Continue on until the end of the lane and then turn left to head down a narrow, enclosed footway that emerges at a gate above the river. Go through the gate and, bearing to the right, follow the well used path through two fields to reach the visible suspension bridge that lies ahead. **GR 032 989.**

2. Cross the bridge over the Swale and, following the signpost 'Harkerside ½ mile', go straight ahead making for a distant wall but when you reach some scrubby trees and the end of a fence, bear slightly to the right to cross a sleeper bridge and come to a track. Turn right to follow the track past a short section of wall and at the end of it, turn slightly to the right to a small gate with a bridleway marker post alongside it. Pass through the gate and follow the grass track as it crosses diagonally across the field making for the river. The track comes to the riverbank just in front of a wooden gate, pass through the gate and then follow the river upstream on the obvious path.

Eventually you will come to a gate in a wooden fence which is opposite the village of Healaugh which sits on the other side of the river. Hear a bridleway sign

Walking beside the Swale.

on the gatepost points the path up and away from the riverbank to join the wall on the left as it goes up the bank. Stay with the wall until you come to a small gate, there are blue painted arrows on the wall after the gate indicating that the bridleway goes straight on. However, ignore these and turn left to go straight through the gate and then through a series of gates on the right of the buildings of Stubbin Farm to emerge in front of the farm buildings. Here another finger-

The gateway leading up to Stubbin Farm.

post points out the way of the bridleway, straight ahead up a short, steep bank. So ignoring the track on the right, head straight up the bank and as you get higher make for a gate on the left of a small barn in front. Go through this gate and, bearing to the right following the direction shown by the bridleway sign,

46

shortly come to the side of a tarmac road. **GR 019 983.**

3. Ignore the right of way markers on the roadside and turn left onto the road and follow it until you get to a marker post with both a bridleway and a footpath arm which sits on the right side of the road, next to a track. Don't follow the track indicated by the bridleway sign but instead follow the path shown by the footpath sign, climbing ahead to a lone tree on the skyline. After a short steep climb you will come to the earthworks of Maiden Castle which are next to the tree. **GR 021 981.** See feature on Maiden Castle for further details.

The footpath sign pointing to the lone tree on the skyline.

Standing in the bottom of the ditch with Calver Hill in the background.

4. Return back to the single tree and continue to follow the original path as it climbs up above Maiden Castle and going to the right of a gully. As you climb, a cairn becomes visible above you on the right, keep going straight up to meet a path that comes from the cairn and runs through the heather along the edge of the hill. Turn left to follow the path, although narrow and, at certain times of the year, overgrown with heather it is still fairly easy to follow. Stay on the path for about 400 metres to come to a junction with another narrow path coming down from the hillside above you. Care is needed at this junction as it can be easily missed. **GR 025 980.**

5. Turn right onto this path and start to follow it uphill and, after about 30 metres, look over to the right to a spread of stones laid out in the heather.

When you get across to them you'll see that the stones are laid out in a ring. These are the foundations of a hut circle dating back to the iron age, over two thousand years ago, and would have formed part of the settlements on Harkerside, probably owing allegiance to the local rulers in Maiden Castle.

The Iron Age hut circle seen from the path above.

Detail of the hut's stone walls.

Continue on the path for a short climb to the top of the rise and here leave the path, which continues on over the level ground before starting uphill again, to turn left onto a very faint path and follow it as it makes it's way along the edge of the ridge. After a short while you'll come to a junction with a grass track that is coming down from the hill on the right. Turn left to follow this track downhill and as you go past a concrete pond, the track bends to the right to go through a line of grouse butts and head towards a distant wall. When the track arrives at the wall, you'll find a wire fence with a gate and a track running through it. **GR 031 981.**

6. Don't go through the gate, instead turn right on to the track and start to follow it as it goes uphill. After a short distance the wall on the left turns away and at this point a faint, grassy path leaves the track on the left hand side. Leave the track and follow this path, as you get into the heather the path gets more pronounced and easier to follow. After a while, a wall comes in from the left and the path starts to run alongside it and shortly after this you'll come to a fence and gate. **GR 039 977.**

7. Go through the gate and continue to follow the path until you come to a junction with another grassy path that heads off downhill to the left. Just to aid identification, there is a rather prominent stone, full of holes, in the middle of the track. At this junction, take the left fork to head downhill. After a short distance you'll come to another junction in the grassy path, again take the left fork to continue going downhill, now down towards the walls below you. As you descend, a wire fence will become visible in front and the path will come to a gate in this fence. Go through the gate and continue on the grassy path which as you descend becomes more of a track and bears to the right. Pass through the next gate and enter a lane which winds between a couple of houses and crosses a bridge to arrive at the roadside. **GR 046 981.**

8. Turn left onto the road and descend into Grinton and here cross the bridge over the Swale. On the other side, on the left hand side of the road, a footpath goes down some steps and into the meadows. Turn off the road and follow the path across a couple of meadows, in the second one follow the well used and newly fenced path as it bears to the right and then heads to the left of Fremington Mill Farm to run along the side of the Arkle Beck. The path emerges onto the roadside where you turn left to cross Reeth Bridge and head back to the green and suitable refreshment.

MAIDEN CASTLE

There are a number of defended sites, or 'hill-forts' as they are more popularly known, within Swaledale. None of these have been excavated although they all date back to the late Bronze or Iron Age, from about 1,000 BC to the time of the Roman invasion.

Of these settlements the one standing on Harkerside, known as Maiden Castle, is probably the most well known. The name 'Maiden Castle' seems to come from the Celtic 'mai-dun', meaning a ridge reflecting the positioning of these sites in elevated positions.

Positioned on a shoulder of a hill on Harkerside, Maiden Castle is one of the most unusual forts in the country both due to it's positioning and it's unique stone entrance corridor. Most hill-forts are on well-defined hills, but this one actually lies on a hill slope, overlooked by higher ground a short distance away. Strategically this is a very poor position as it would be easy for an enemy to fire down onto the defenders within the fort and this does tend to suggest that it's main purpose was not military.

Similar to Calver Hill on the other side of the valley, during the late Bronze and Iron Age Harkerside was home to an extensive coaxial field wall system which appears to stop just short of the castle's earthworks and within these field patterns are traces of round houses and settlements. Maybe Maiden Castle was the headquarters or the main house of the settlements, the equivalent of the Lord of the Manor. It may also be possible that the other, smaller defended settlements in the locality may have been subservient to Maiden Castle.

The ditch and ramparts running past the single tree.

50

The structure is quite elaborate with the site fitting neatly into the hill rather than standing on top of it. The earthworks and stone ramparts are quite sizeable with the enclosure itself measuring 140 metres x 120 metres. This site took a lot of man-hours to complete and for this much effort, it must have had some significance.

Starting from the east, a collapsed stone corridor of two parallel walls leads for 110 metres to the entrance of the enclosure. At it's highest, where they join onto the enclosure, the walls of this corridor must have stood possibly 4 metres (13 feet) high. There is a structure built into the walls but this appears to be a more recent grouse butt.

The stone entrance corridor with tumulus in the background.

The enclosure itself is more pear-shaped than round and, as stated above, covers a large area. The site is defined by massive earthworks comprising a ditch, in places up to 4 metres deep and 10 metres wide. Within the ditch circle lies a rubble wall with coursed dry stone facing. No excavation work has ever been done on Maiden Castle and it is not known how tall the wall would have stood when newly built although it is quite possible that it would have been topped with a wooden palisade or even stone ramparts.

Inside the earthworks lies a large flat area which would have been the settlement. Inbuilt to the southern side of the rampart walls lies the remains of two stone structures, in all probability the footings of two round houses. There is also evidence of two further platforms, areas of flat ground on which the houses were built, somewhere among the heather but you are unlikely to find those.

Descending down into the main settlement area.
Below, one of the two hut circles built into the southern ramparts seen from above and detail of the footings of the hut.

Maiden Castle is not the largest defended settlement in Swaledale, that honour goes to a very damaged hill-fort on How Hill near the village of Downholme further down the valley. However it is the largest of the defended sites in Upper Swaledale and is the only one that is accessible to the curious walker. Two of the other sites, at Grinton and close to Scabba Wath Bridge, are passed on other walks in this book.

One local tradition refers to a tumulus, or burial mound, which is situated close to the start of the entrance corridor which, dating back to the Bronze Age, is even older than Maiden Castle. According to this local custom, a chest of gold is reputedly buried under this mound. As can be seen from the many holes dug into the side of it, one or two people have tried searching for it over the years. All to no avail.

52

The Neolithic walled enclosure on Cringley Hill.
Walk 5: The Enclosures of Calver.

WALK 5: THE ENCLOSURES OF CALVER

Calver Hill rises directly behind Reeth and for many walkers it's summit is an obvious objective for a walk. However, how many walkers know the true history of this hill and the landscape that surrounds it. Hidden beneath the boots of the walker are some of the most extensive remains of our prehistoric past within the region. Dating back 4,000 years to the Bronze Age and even further to the Neolithic, this part of Swaledale was home to a very civilised culture. This walk takes you on a discovery to find the villages and farms of our ancient ancestors.

This is a medium length walk that in principle shouldn't take you long but for those who enjoy exploring the past there is such a wealth of sites and points of interest on this walk that it can take a lot longer than expected. You will also find yourself wandering across the open moor locating different sites among the heather and in some cases wandering backwards and forwards across the moor but not, I stress, aimlessly. Well hopefully !

DISTANCE: 7.6 miles (12.1 km)
ASCENT: 1,240 feet (378 metres)
TERRAIN: Because on this walk you are following a trail between prehistoric monuments which, in the main, aren't conveniently located next to footpaths then you will be doing a fair amount of walking off-path. However, Calver is not particularly a wild hill and is mainly covered with moor grass so this doesn't present much of a problem. The track that is used at the start and finish of the walk to access the open moor, Skelgate Lane, is badly eroded and quite stony underfoot, it can also be quite wet in poor weather. In the early stages of the walk, the climb up to the summit of Calver is quite steep.
TIME: 4 to 5 hours.
START: Reeth Village Green. GR SE 038 992
DOGS: As most of this walk is off public rights of way and over open access land including a bit of 'wandering about' then it would be best not to bring your dog on this walk.
ACCESS: Most of this walk is away from public rights of way and over open access land.

Grid References:

Reeth village green	038 992
Top of Skelgate	029 998
Track/path junction	026 997
Calver summit	013 003
Cairns	006 003
Neolithic enclosure	002 005
Hut circle	005 006
Track junction	004 009
Track junction	994 009
Cairns	998 005
Track junction	000 001
Settlement	999 002
Track junction	007 999
Track/path junction	016 996
Reeth village green	038 992

FGS Grading

Grading is F7 [D1, N1, T2, R1, H2]

Distance	1	6 – 12 miles
Navigation	**1**	Basic navigation skills needed
Terrain	**2**	25 -50% on graded track or path 50 – 75% off track
Remoteness	**1**	Countryside in fairly close proximity to habitation – at least 80% of the route within 2 miles
Height	**2**	Over 125 ft per mile

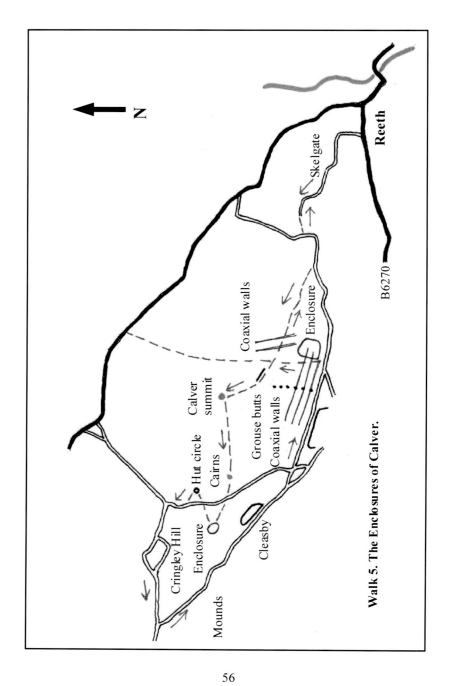

Walk 5. The Enclosures of Calver.

N

Reeth

B6270

Skelgate

Coaxial walls

Enclosure

Calver summit

Grouse butts

Coaxial walls

Hut circle

Cairns

Enclosure

Cringley Hill

Cleasby

Mounds

THE WALK

1. Leave the green and follow the B6270 as it heads out of the village towards Gunnerside further up the dale. Follow the footpath on the right side of the road and just after leaving the village come to a walled lane on the right with a signpost "Skellgate". Turn right to follow the lane as it makes it's long way up to the gate leading onto the open moor. **GR 029 998.**

2. Go through the gate and follow the path straight ahead, passing a small cairn, to join a track just where it bends. Turn left on to the track and follow it for 150 metres (about 165 paces) to where the wall on the left comes up to run next to the track. Here a very faint quad bike track leaves the right side of the track to head towards the top of Calver Hill. **GR 026 997.**

Calver Hill rises up prominently behind Reeth. Originally pronounced Calvay, the name means 'the calves hedged enclosure' and probably refers back to the practice of grazing stock on these low moors.

3. Leave the track to follow this faint path as it climbs steadily over Riddings Rigg, it does get more distinctive after a short distance and passes to the right of a small quarry. As you walk keep your eyes open for a number of lines of low stone mounds.

These are the remains of co-axial boundary walls dating back to the Bronze

Coaxial walls, recognised by the lines of large stones running across the moor.

Age. There are a couple of distinct field systems running over these moors but we will look at these in more detail later.

Follow the path and as it climbs, it approaches a partially collapsed stone wall that runs up the face of Calver.

Looking back down the line of the bield.

It may seem strange to have a standalone stretch of walling running over the moor. This is what is known as a bield, one of a number on this moor above Reeth. They were built to provide shelter for sheep during inclement weather, the age of this one is not known but most of those on the moor are over a couple of hundred years old.

On the left side of the wall is a path, which although steep, provides the easiest way up to the summit cairn of Calver. **GR 013 003.**

4. From the summit cairn follow the left side of the hill to descend down to two cairns. **GR 006 003.**

The more prominent cairn is a modern construction but the smaller one lying slightly to the north west is what is left of a Bronze Age cairn. Dating back almost four thousand years, the cairn was estimated to have been around ten metres in diameter, over thirty feet, when complete but over the years and like so many similar ones, has been robbed for its stone. The placing of the cairn up here on the shoulder of Calver, high above the field systems and settlements on the terraces below was highly significant as the cairn was not just the resting place of somebody revered by the community but was also a highly visible territorial marker.

5. From the cairn continue heading westward down into the col between Calver and Cringley Hill to cross a track coming up from the Swaledale side of the hill. At this point you pick up a faint path that heads up to Cringley. After 200 metres and on the top of the rise, you'll pass the low stone walls of a Neolithic enclosure which lies to the right of the path. **GR 002 005.**

The enclosure found here is thought to date back to the Neolithic and has given the name Cringley Hill, coming from the Old Norse "kringla" meaning a circle. Situated on the saddle between Cringley Hill and Calver Hill this enclosure probably dates back over four thousand years. Nowadays we see this spot as relatively high peat moorland but at that time these hills would have been wooded with oak, ash and elm, with the area around this enclosure being cleared of trees to provide rich grazing for the early domesticated cattle.

This roughly circular enclosure is one of the earliest examples of human settlement in the dale even though it may have been only seasonal settlement as the early farmers migrated seeking new pastures with their animals. The enclosure is defended by a substantial stone wall 1.2 metres (4 feet) thick. Many of the stones have since been removed by quarrying and to build more modern walls but the outer facings of the wall can still be seen as can the stone core which was made up of smaller packing stones. It is probable that the wall may not have been that high but may have been topped by some form of hedge to help contain livestock and protect them from predators such as wolves, wildcats and bears. Try walking round the outline of the walls to get an idea of their layout.

The walls of the Neolithic enclosure on Cringley Hill.

6. From the northern side of the enclosure head on a compass bearing of 80 degrees for approximately 300 paces and as you do so pass over the same green track that you crossed when descending from Calver. The area of moor here is relatively small and so to go from artefact to artefact you do tend to criss-cross the moor. At the end of the 300 paces you'll be in an area of burial mounds. Although the OS map describes this as a "hut circle" the size and structure more closely resemble the remains of an excavated burial mound. **GR 005 006.**

Marked on the OS map as a hut circle this ring of stones more closely resemble the remains of a burial mound from the Bronze Age.

7. From the hut circle go back to the green track that you seem to keep crossing and turn right to follow it down towards the Arkengarthdale side of the ridge. After 300 metres the track will meet a well constructed vehicle track. **GR 004 009.**

8. Turn left to follow this new track as it slowly climbs round the side of Cringley Hill and ignore the two minor tracks on the left that lead up to an old limestone quarry, and stay on the obvious main track.

Even earlier than the Neolithic, during the Mesolithic when the scattered population of this country were just roaming hunter/gatherers, this area was a valuable source of food. A flint chipping floor, a site where hunting tools were fashioned and repaired, possibly as part of a hunting encampment, has been found here.

Continue following the track until just before you reach a gate, there is a junction with another less pronounced track that runs in on the left alongside a wall. **GR 994 009.**

9. Turn left to follow the track next to the wall. The track climbs steadily as it stays close to the side of Cringley Hill but soon levels out and the closeness of the hill starts to open out as the hillside on the left curves away. As the track starts to descend a green hillside becomes visible about 200 metres away on the left. At this point on the right side of the track the remains of a long barrow, a form of burial mound, and other cairn mounds, created from the clearance of early fields, lie on the side of the track. **GR 998 005.**

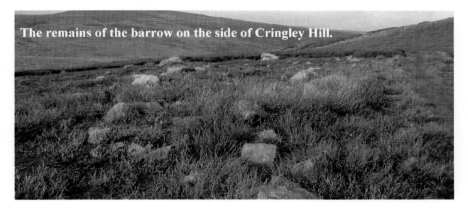

The remains of the barrow on the side of Cringley Hill.

10. Continue following the track as it curves to head downhill. As the track descends it passes on the left a square enclosure comprised of banks and stones

Identified from aerial photographs, this enclosure is seen as a potential prehistoric settlement although no dating or excavating work has yet been completed on it.
At the bottom of the hill the track comes to a T-junction. **GR 000 001.**

11. Turn right for a small out and back diversion, the track immediately starts to climb again but instead of following it stay close to the outside of the walls where you'll find a Bronze Age settlement site comprising cleared areas, walling, clearance cairns, an oval hut platform and a robbed cairn. Within this area is also a ring cairn and the fragments of a possible standing stone. **GR 999 002.**

12. Turn round and head back to the junction and from there follow the track as it makes its way along the side of the hill, passing underneath the more modern walled enclosure known as Cleasby. The remains of a second Neolithic enclosure have been found lying to the east of Cleasby, unfortunately there is not sufficient of this structure visible to warrant looking for it. Continue on the track until you come to a junction with another track coming down from the side of Calver. **GR 007 999.**

13. Ignore this side track and continue making your way below the slopes of Calver. After around 600 metres you'll start to see a line of stone grouse butts ahead. As you get closer look to the left and a short distance up the hill a line of white stones has been revealed by heather burning. Make your way across the heather to the stones which are the remains of one of the coaxial field boundaries found running across Calverside. At this point, partially due to the heather

Looking up to the coaxial wall.

burning, the line of the wall is easily distinguished. A quick compass bearing will establish that it runs on a line of 110 degrees across the hillside and if you walk along the line towards the grouse butts you will meet the track again.

Continue following the track as it starts to make its way downhill to join a well-constructed dirt road. Just before joining the track you'll pass between the remains of two old lead mining shafts, one on either side of the track. Turn left onto the track and after a couple of metres come to a signpost indicating a footpath heading off up the side of the hill. **GR 016 996.**

14. Turn onto the footpath and as you follow it up the hill, count your steps. Depending on stride length, after approx 290 paces you'll find a small stone cairn on the right side of the path. At this point leave the path and go to the right and after, literally, a metre or two you'll find the low stone earthworks forming an enclosure.

This circular enclosure is overlain by a wall from one of the two co-axial walls on this part of the moor. As these co-axial walls are known to date to the Bronze Age then the enclosure must be earlier, possibly Neolithic.

On the uphill side of the enclosure you'll find the line of the co-axial wall. A

The coaxial wall approaching the grouse butts.

check on the compass will confirm that this wall also runs on a bearing of 110 degrees, the same as the previous wall next to the grouse butts. In fact this wall runs across the moor exactly parallel to the first. The line of the wall can be followed westwards, back across the path towards the face of Calver. At GR 015 999 a small round platform set into the hill is the location of a round house that resided in this enclosure.

15. From this location, the uppermost grouse butts from the line of butts that were passed earlier are easily visible a short distance away. Just past the butts there is a knoll on which there a sheep bield, similar to the one encountered while climbing Calver, and from here the lines of both the co-axial walls can be seen.

Imagine both these walls as they existed in the Bronze Age. Low and wide, these squat walls would have had hedges running along the top of them. In-between the two walls would have been a long, wide grazing area of grassland running across the hillside, full of early domesticated long horn cattle. The small roundhouse set against the northern wall would have provided shelter for the herders.

16. From the knoll retrace your steps past the remains of the round house and back along the line of the wall. When you get back to the footpath heading up the hill, turn left to follow it as it climbs the slopes. At the top you'll come to the same stone bield wall that you encountered on the walk up to Calver. From here turn right to retrace your steps across the moor to the top of Skelgate and then follow the lane down to Reeth.

EARLY LIFE ON CALVER HILL.

The moorlands surrounding Reeth have been used since the earliest times. Evidence of Mesolithic hunter/gatherers, such as arrow heads and flint tools, that date back over six thousand years have been found in a number of places within the dale. However, it isn't until the start of agriculture in the Neolithic, over four thousand years ago, that these scattered tribes people started to establish semi-permanent settlements on the hillsides. In these early days they were probably seasonal, tied in with the migration of livestock and the growing season. The population moving up from lower lying areas from May to early November before moving back for the winter.

Evidence of this early settlement has been found in the form of leaf-shaped arrow heads, a characteristic Neolithic shape, discovered on the slopes of Calver Hill. However, the most striking evidence is in the walls of two enclosures found on the flanks of the hill, one on Cringley Hill and the other on Riddings Rigg, the eastern shoulder of Calver.

At this time the landscape was markedly different to the open moorland that we see today. The climate was warmer and these hills, now covered by peat and heather, were then wooded by a mix of oak, ash, alder and elm trees.

By the time that the Neolithic had started to merge in to what is now called the Bronze Age, the inhabitants had become more settled and the hills around Reeth were entering a lengthy stage of development. During this phase settlements

Following the line of a Bronze Age field wall on the side of Cringley Hill.

were becoming more permanent with little groups of round houses sitting on the sides of the hills grouped around small field enclosures. Field walls were starting to be constructed, probably from stones that were being cleared from the fields. The shape of these fields were fairly irregular and often marked by small clearance cairns, mounds of stones thrown to one side while the fields were being cleared for cultivation.

From these early beginnings an organised, planned landscape developed that existed through many centuries from the Bronze Age, through the Iron Age and was probably still in use long after the Roman occupation had started. As in many other parts of the country, the use of very substantial stone banks as field boundaries was adopted. These are known as coaxial field systems as their main boundaries run parallel or coaxial.

The coaxial walls that formed the boundaries were low stone banks made by dumped stone in-between two rows of facing stones. These are quite substantial measuring between one and three metres in width and almost one metre high. They were then topped with a hedge, these walls were more like hedge banks than the stone walls surrounding the fields of today, but they did form a substantial barrier to both contain and control livestock.

Coaxial walls on the side of Calver.

As in other parts of the country, notably Dartmoor, these coaxial walls were extensive. On the hillside above Reeth, a series of straight, parallel walls ran for 3.5 kms across the south facing slopes of Cringley Hill, Riddings Rigg and Black Hill and possibly extended even further down to the Swale flood plain although any evidence has been lost due to reuse of the land for more modern field systems plus mining and quarrying during the 17th, 18th and 19th centuries. The walls ran in long, straight lines across the landscape irrespective of any obstacles, crossing any streams and gullies in their way and running up the slopes of the hills.

As the settlements developed into the Iron Age, large swathes of countryside was opened up to agriculture throughout the north of England. Pollen analysis has shown that during this timeframe the main pollen groups changed from trees and similar vegetation to those of the grasses indicating a wide spread expansion of farming. From the Middle Iron Age, through to the Late and into Roman time, Swaledale was supporting a very high population density, much higher than the dale of today.

But things change and since the Bronze and Iron Age the general climate of these uplands has deteriorated bringing changes to the soil cover of the hills. The soil is now more acid and that plus a colder, wetter climate has led to a more extensive and deeper peat cover on the hills. Land that was once suitable for grazing and pasture and would have also been suitable for growing a limited range of crops has, over the centuries, had to be abandoned as the settlements and field systems retreated down the slopes to occupy the lower sides of the dale where the walled pastures are today.

Time Line.

Time can be sometimes hard to grasp especially when talking about the prehistoric and the various different time periods. To give a brief idea of how far back so of these monuments date the generally accepted prehistoric time line is shown below.

Mesolithic	8,000 to 4,000 BC
Neolithic	4,000 to 2,000 BC
Bronze Age	2,200 to 750 BC
Iron Age	750 BC to 43 AD
Roman Occupation	43 to 410 AD

Approaching the shooting hut on Harkerside.

WALK 6: WHITASIDE MOOR & GREEN HILLS

A walk that follows the course of the River Swale upstream, passing as it does so one of the small fortified settlements from the Iron Age that lie on glacial moraines on the valley floor. The route then loops back over Green Hill, passing through several of the numerous mining grounds that line the southern side of the valley, before descending back down to the river to return to Reeth.

DISTANCE: 9.7 miles (15.5 km)
ASCENT: 1,093 feet (333 metres)
TERRAIN: This route comprises riverside and field paths, a walled lane and well-surfaced moorland tracks. From Low Houses there is a fairly steep climb up the side of the valley through rough field pasture. Approximately 700 metres of this route is along the main valley road which at times may be busy. The

route also uses stepping stones to cross the Barney Beck and in times of bad weather/high water levels these stones may not be accessible and a diversion may have to be made through the village of Healaugh and along the main road.

TIME: 4 to 5 hours.

START: Reeth Village Green. GR SE 038 992

DOGS: As the route is all on rights of way then dogs are allowed, however, do keep them under close control. The walk passes through or close to three farm-yards and other dogs may be encountered here, livestock ranging from chickens to sheep and cattle will also met on this route. A 700 metre stretch of the main valley road is followed in the early stages of the walk.

ACCESS: The route is all on public rights of way although there may be small sections on the moor where the track does not quite mirror the right of way as shown on the OS map. However, as the moors are all access land there should be no problem over these little 'wobbles'.

Grid references:

Reeth village green	038 992
Scabba Wath Bridge	006 983
Low House Farm	982 973
Track/road junction	986 967
Road/track junction	983 964
Track junction	987 958
Track junction	012 972
Track/road junction	020 983
Reeth village green	038 992

FGS Grading

Grading is F4 [D1, N1, T0, R1, H1]

Distance	1	6 – 12 miles
Navigation	1	Basic navigation skills needed
Terrain	0	75% + on graded track or path
Remoteness	1	Countryside in fairly close proximity to habitation – at least 80% of the route within 2 miles
Height	1	Over 100 ft per mile

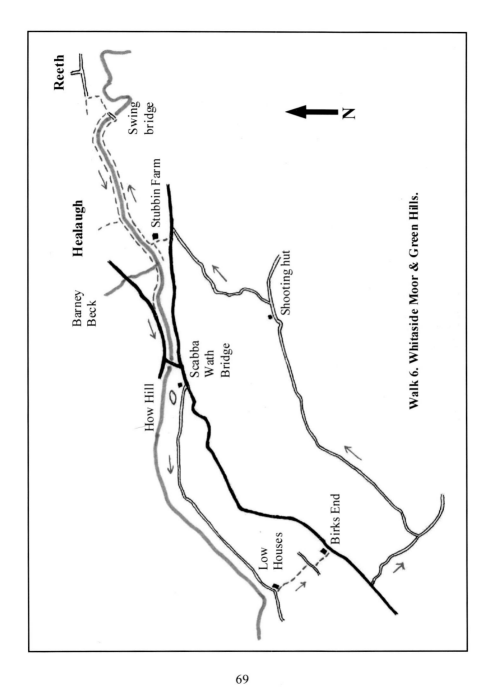

Reeth

Swing bridge

Healaugh

Stubbin Farm

Barney Beck

Scabba Wath Bridge

How Hill

Shooting hut

Low Houses

Birks End

N

Walk 6. Whitaside Moor & Green Hills.

69

THE WALK

1. From Reeth descend down to the river and the swing bridge using the same route as Walks 2 and 4 but instead of crossing the bridge continue straight ahead to follow the riverside path upstream with the river on your left. After you have left the bridge, the path continues through the trees along the riverbank and is a little bit upsy-downsy in places due to riverbank erosion. Around 300 metres later you'll come to a path junction marked with a signpost, you'll need to bear left through the small gate to continue on the riverside path even though this is not marked on the signpost. After a while you'll pass large stepping stones across the river, dependant upon how high the river is flowing, and here pass another junction with a path on the right that goes up to the village of Healaugh.

This is the point where if the weather is bad and you can't cross the Barney Beck, you need to return to and go up to Healaugh before turning left to follow the road to Scabba Wath Bridge.

Continue following the river to come to the mouth of the Barney Beck as it enters the Swale.

Stepping stones over the Barney Beck.

Cross via the stepping stones and continue on the path by the river. After a short distance, a fence will appear on the left and a stile will lead through a small patch of woodland to exit out onto the roadside. Here turn left and, taking care of the traffic, follow the road until you come to the Askrigg turning on the left and go down here to Scabba Wath Bridge. **GR 006 983**.

Also known as Low Whita Bridge, Scabba Wath Bridge lies a little upstream from the old ford that it replaced. The word "Wath" derives from the Old Scandinavian word 'Vath' meaning ford and for many centuries before this old bridge was built, there was a ford across the Swale. At one time the ford was a part of the Roman road that linked the fort at Bainbridge in Wensleydale to the one at Bowes.

2. Cross the bridge and at the road junction on the other side turn right to follow the road for 200 metres, past the farm buildings, to where the road turns sharply left uphill. Here leave the road to turn right down the track marked 'Low Row Bunk House' and after a metre or so pass a footpath sign to 'Low Houses'. Go past the bunk house to enter a walled lane which is now followed for just over 2 km but before you do have a look over the wall on the right to the small hill lying between you and the river.

How Hill is formed from glacial moraine, rock and stone left behind as the glaciers retreated at the end of the last Ice Age. There are several of these small hills laid along the valley floor of the dale. Like the similar hill at Grinton on Walk 3, How Hill was utilised by the Iron Age Celts as a place to build a fortified settlement. The characteristic remains of earthworks can be easily seen circling the top of the hill, these defences would have been formed from a ditch and bank, possibly topped with a wooden palisade.

How Hill defended settlement.

Continue following the walled lane, navigation is quite easy as, quite simply, there is nowhere else to go. The track itself, climbs very slowly to the point where you don't even realise that you are climbing until you look down to the river below and notice that you are quite a way above it. Eventually the lane exits out onto the head of a tarmac road at Low Houses Farm. **GR 982 973**.

3. Turn right for a few metres to go past the farm buildings on the left and immediately after the metal barn there is a gate with a broken bridleway sign stuck on the top of the stone wall, see photo right.

71

Go through the gate and follow the bridleway up a sunken track as it climbs quite steeply up the side of the hill. As this sunken track starts to bear away to the right continue straight ahead passing on the left of the telegraph pole and making for the single tree at the top of the slope. Pass on the left of the tree and continue climbing straight ahead up the field. The OS map shows the right of way running alongside the wall on the right, although in reality, the path tends to go up the middle of the field and so, as you near the wall at the top of the field, you need to bear right to go through a gateway in the right hand wall to join onto a walled lane. Turn right to follow the lane a short distance to a junction just before a shallow ford and here turn left to continue climbing past Birk End Farm to arrive at the roadside. **GR 986 967**.

As you walk up the track towards Birk End Farm, the small building in ruins to the right of the track is what is left of a small two-roomed cottage dating back to the 1700's. The steep slope of the gables show that it had a thatched roof, with the thatch material being heather gathered off the moors. In Swaledale thatched roofs were still the norm until the mid to late 1700's.

If you fancy a break for lunch and a cuppa then you wouldn't find better places than sitting on the parapet of the bridge. The views up the valley take some beating.

4. Turn right onto the road and follow it for 500 metres until, just past a stone-built shed on the left side of the road, you'll come to a track, again on the left. Hidden behind the access land notices is a direction fingerpost pointing the way to Castle Bolton. **GR 983 964**.

5. Leave the road and head up the track as it makes it's way up the side of the hill. After a short distance and just as the track bends to the left, a side track heads off to the right making for the inevitable group of spoil heaps that can be seen over there. Stay on the main track as it now starts to move through the Whitaside mining grounds. As it slowly climbs it passes a number of hushes and spoil heaps although the main mines and shafts are a little bit further over to the right. Amongst the spoil heaps you'll come to a junction with another track coming in from the left. **GR 987 958**.

6. Turn left and follow the track as it heads to and around the side of Green Hills. After just over 1 km you'll pass a cairn a little distance away on the left on the shoulder of the hill and you'll then start to descend Green Hill Ends. Stay

The old lime kiln next to the track.

on the track to pass an old lime kiln built into the remains of quite a large hush. After what seems a very long time you will eventually come to a large shooting hut and shortly after that a junction with another track on the left. **GR 012 972**.

7. Turn left to follow this track downhill past the remains of the Harker lead mines over on the right. The track twists and turns it's way downhill to eventually arrive at the roadside. **GR 020 983**.

8. Turn left and follow the road down for a short distance until you come to a bridleway signpost on the left side of the road. Here leave the road and turn right to follow the direction shown by the sign and drop down over the rough ground to the wooden gate on the right of the stone barn. Pass through the gate and then follow the path in front as it bears slightly to the right before heading down to the left hand gate in front of the farm and here you will find a bridleway sign. Go straight ahead through the gate and then through the gates to the left of the farm buildings. You will then come to another gate that takes you into a short walled lane and once through the gate at the other end, turn right to follow the wall and descend down to the river. Now turn right to follow the riverside path downstream to come back to the swing bridge, cross and bear right to return to Reeth.

Surrender Smelt Mill above the Barney Beck.

WALK 7: SURRENDER SMELT MILL & THE BARNEY BECK

There are many old smelt mills in Swaledale covering the various mining grounds, sometimes these may be quite close together reflecting the different ownership of the various mines.

This walk visits one of these mills that is set on the banks of the Barney Beck above Healaugh. This is one of the better preserved mills in the dale and with it's long flue snaking up the side of the hill, presents a fascinating insight into the days of the lead miner.

DISTANCE: 7.2 miles (11.5 km)
ASCENT: 853 feet (260 metres)
TERRAIN: A mix of field and moorland tracks and paths. There are two short steep descents down to stream crossings and then two steep climbs back up on the opposite side. The stream crossings are, under normal conditions, fairly easy

74

to get over. However, in wet weather they can be quite hazardous and should not be attempted. In bad weather it would be prudent to choose another walk. There are a couple of short road sections in and out of Healaugh.

TIME: 4½ to 5 hours.

START: Reeth Village Green. GRSE 038 992

DOGS: Dogs are ok on this walk but be aware that there are some really awkward stiles to get them across plus at one point there is a steep drop, off to the right above the Barney Beck. In summer the section above the Barney Beck also gets very overgrown with bracken, not very pleasant walking for your dog. Sheep will be encountered throughout the walk.

ACCESS: The route uses a combination of rights of way and public access land. Although the route is all on well established tracks and paths, not all of these are rights of way and some of the paths that are do not necessarily match the right of way as shown by the OS map.

Grid references:

Reeth village green	038 992
Healaugh	019 991
Thirns Farm	012 995
Track junction	010 996
Track junction	005 000
Stile in wall	996 002
Surrender Smelt Mill	990 999
Track/road junction	015 989
Healaugh	019 991
Reeth village green	038 992

FGS Grading

Grading is F5 [D1, N1, T1, R1, H1]

Distance	1	6 – 12 miles
Navigation	1	Basic navigation skills needed
Terrain	1	50 – 75% on graded track or path 25 – 50% off track
Remoteness	1	Countryside in fairly close proximity to habitation – at least 80% of the route within 2 miles
Height	1	Over 100 ft per mile

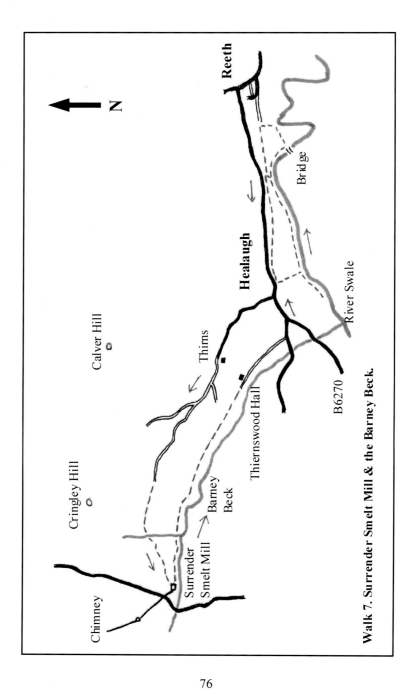

N

Reeth

Bridge

Healaugh

River Swale

Calver Hill

Thirns

Thiernswood Hall

B6270

Cringley Hill

Barney Beck

Surrender Smelt Mill

Chimney

Walk 7. Surrender Smelt Mill & the Barney Beck.

THE WALK

1. From the green, head past the King's Arms and Black Bull pubs to come to the small green at Anvil square. Pass the green and following the sign 'To the river', which is high up the wall of The Garden House, go down a small lane between the walls. As the lane emerges onto a narrow road, go straight ahead to come to a street where you turn left for a short distance to come to a T-junction. Turn right to follow the signs 'Swing Bridge' and 'Doctors Surgery' and head down the narrow lane passing the surgery on the way. At the last house, Quakers Garth, the tarmac ends and the surface becomes unmetaled. Continue on until the end of the lane and here, ignore the lane on the left and go through the small walker's gate to the right of the main gate in front. There is a footpath signpost hidden in the hedge showing that this is the way to Healaugh.

There is an old sunken way next to the wall on the left which is what the footpath follows although most walker's follow the obvious level way straight ahead for a short distance before dropping down to the left to join the original route. Make for an obvious stile in the wall corner and from here it is an easy task of following the well walked path straight across the fields making for the stiles on the opposite side. The majority of these stiles have large daubs of yellow paint on them making them easy to spot. As you near Healaugh the path passes an old barn on the left and here the field slopes away down to the left with the path going ahead but curving slightly to the right across the slope of the hill to come to another stile built into the field wall.

The path running across the slope of the hill as you approach Healaugh.

Go across another couple of fields to exit out onto the green in Healaugh. **GR 019 991**.

Although it might seem quiet and unassuming now, especially when compared to Reeth, in years past Healaugh was the dominant village in Swaledale. After the Conquest and the appropriation of Anglo-Saxon land by the new Norman lords, Healaugh was the head of the extensive Manor of Healaugh, an estate of some 40,000 acres covering most of Swaledale. During this time the whole area was quite heavily forested, the village name derives from the Anglian word 'Helagh' meaning stronghold in a forest clearing. Nowadays the only length of wooded land lies along the valley of the Barney Beck.

2. Start to follow the main road through the village and then turn right to follow a tarmac lane past West View cottage. Stay on the lane as it leaves the village, going through the gate across the road and starts climbing up to the open moor. When you get to the top of the bank, ignore the footpath signpost in front of you and stay on the tarmac track. Shortly before you reach Thirns Farm you'll pass an old heather-thatched barn on the left.

The restored thatched barn here is a flashback to earlier days. Prior to the early 1800's, the majority of buildings in the dale were thatched be it barn or cottage. A boom in the lead industry during the early part of the 19th century led to many alterations in the miner's cottages with most having a second storey added and the thatch being replaced with stone flags to form the image of 'traditional' Swaledale.

Not long after this you'll come to Thirns Farm where the tarmac ends. **GR 012 995**.

3. Ignore the track on the right and continue straight on following the track along the outside of the wall. After 150/200 metres you'll come to a junction (**GR 010 996**) where you leave the well-made track and turn right onto a slightly rougher track which at first climbs and then bends to continue straight ahead. Follow this to and then around the right side of a large field enclosure and then straight ahead to come to another track junction (**GR 005 000**). Here there is a fallen way marker post laid on the ground which at some point may be re-erected and the walls of a large enclosure called Cleasby are over to the right. Continue on the obvious main track to eventually come to a ruined building, a wall and a fence. Go through the gateway and the track now becomes more of a path but continue following it along the right side of the wall. After a short distance you'll come to a cross-wall in front with a stile in the wall corner. **GR 996 002**.

4. Cross the stile and bear to the right to follow the path as it descends quite steeply to cross the stream in the gully bottom. The path going up the other side is quite obvious and is a steep little climb. When you get to the top the path continues to be fairly obvious plus there is the occasional cairn to make the way across the moor. It's not long before the remains of the Surrender Smelt Mill and it's peat store come into view and if it's a nice sunny day you can also see the cars at the parking space above Surrender Bridge. The path passes within a couple of metres of the remains of the peat store so it is an easy matter of crossing over to there and then down to the smelt mill. **GR 990 999**.

Take some time exploring the smelt mill, it is in a fairly good state of preservation and there are information boards explaining the layout and what activities happened here. For those that have a particular interest, the old flue can be easily followed up the side of the hill to come to the remains of a chimney located half-way up it's length.

Built in 1841, the Surrender Smelt Mill replaced two earlier smelt mills that had stood on the same site. In it's day it was quite cutting-edge, having three hearths for smelting the lead out of the ore and a further slag hearth for reprocessing waste, all of these powered by a central waterwheel and bellows

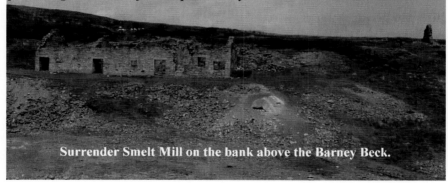

Surrender Smelt Mill on the bank above the Barney Beck.

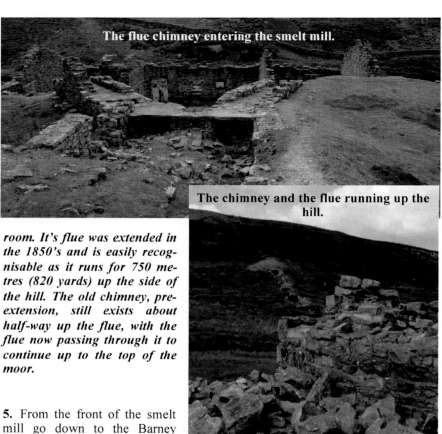

The flue chimney entering the smelt mill.

The chimney and the flue running up the hill.

room. It's flue was extended in the 1850's and is easily recognisable as it runs for 750 metres (820 yards) up the side of the hill. The old chimney, pre-extension, still exists about half-way up the flue, with the flue now passing through it to continue up to the top of the moor.

5. From the front of the smelt mill go down to the Barney beck and follow the left bank downstream. At one point, as the path rises up over the shoulder of the hill, it looks as if it might become a little precarious but it is actually a lot easier walking than it looks and soon descends back down to the side of the stream again. After a short distance you'll come to the stream that you crossed earlier flows down to enter the Barney Beck. Under normal conditions there are plenty of stones to enable you to make an easy crossing and once over, climb up the bank to a gated stile in a stone wall. Pass through the stile and follow the path keeping the wall on the left. In the height of summer this path is overgrown with ferns and it can be a little bit like beating your way though a jungle but it doesn't last for long. The path doesn't always run alongside the wall, for long stretches it is a couple of feet away but eventually you'll come to a point where a cross-wall runs in front of you to

80

form an inner wall corner. Here there is a stile in the wall on the left but ignore this and follow the path as it bends right to follow the cross-wall slightly down-hill to come to an outer wall corner. Here turn left to follow the path round the wall and above a steep drop into the valley on the right. Stay following the path alongside the wall until you come to a signpost and a stile that takes you across onto the other side of the wall. Continue in the same direction but now with the wall on your right. Follow the wall through a number of fields to eventually come to a stile leading into a patch of woodland. Go through and, ignoring the path on the right, continue straight ahead to join a track which brings you out of the wood and past Thirnswood Hall. Stay on the track to eventually come to a tarmac road. **GR 015 989**.

Walking through the wood.

6. Turn left to follow the road for a couple of hundred metres to come to the main valley floor road and here turn left again to re-enter the village of Healaugh. Walk through the village to come to the open green area where you came into the village on the outward leg. (**GR 019 991**). From here you have a route choice, you can return to Reeth via the field paths that you used on the way out or alternatively you can turn right just after passing The Manor House to come to a signpost directing you back to Reeth via the riverside. Follow the signpost down to a gate and across a field to the riverbank and here turn left to follow the river downstream to arrive at the swing bridge across the river. Note that at one point you come to a path junction where there is a signpost 'to Reeth - to Swing bridge', just continue following the path alongside the river. When you get to the swing bridge, follow the same path up to Reeth that you have used on a couple of these walks.

Looking down the flue to Grinton How Smelt Mill.

WALK 8: GRINTON HOW SMELT MILL & THE GROVE-BECK MINES

During the course of the walks in this book we've visited a number of lead mining sites. With this walk we take the opportunity to visit the most well preserved smelt mill within the Yorkshire Dales and then continue the walk through some of the mining grounds that supplied the ore to the mill.

DISTANCE: 6.8 miles (10.8 km)
ASCENT: 1,050 feet (320 metres)
TERRAIN: Mainly field and moorland track or path. There is a section walking up a hush but even here there is a well-defined path beneath your feet. The couple of climbs on this walk are more long and steady rather than steep.
TIME: 4 to 5 hours.
START: Reeth Village Green. GR SE 038 992

DOGS: As most of this walk is on public rights of way then dogs are allowed but keep them under close control. The couple of sections that use access land have, to my knowledge, no restrictions on dogs. However, these are in the areas of the old mines and so you would want to keep them on a lead anyway.

ACCESS: A mixture of public rights of way and access land is used for this route.

Grid references:

Reeth village green	038 992
Grinton Bridge	046 985
Path/road junction	054 981
Track/road junction	052 969
Flue	051 965
Grinton Smelt Mill	049 964
Path/road junction	038 962
Road/path junction	039 964
Track junction	033 972
Track/road junction	032 983
Reeth village green	038 992

FGS Grading

Grading is F5 [D1, N1, T0, R1, H2]

Distance	1	6 – 12 miles
Navigation	1	Basic navigation skills needed
Terrain	0	75% + on graded track or path
Remoteness	1	Countryside in fairly close proximity to habitation – at least 80% of the route within 2 miles
Height	2	Over 125 ft per mile

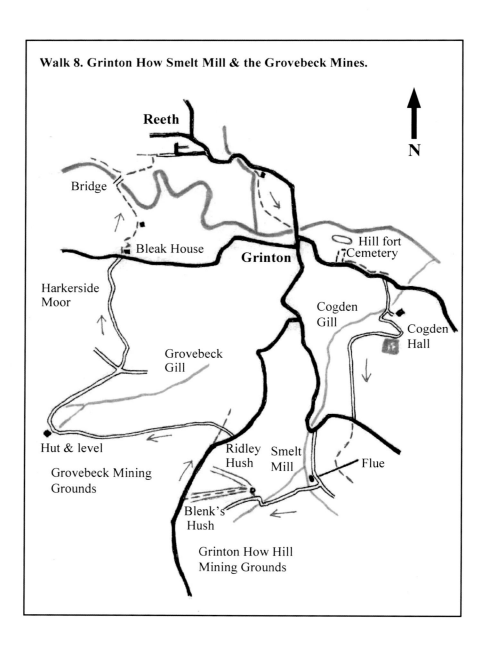

Walk 8. Grinton How Smelt Mill & the Grovebeck Mines.

N

Reeth

Bridge

Bleak House

Grinton

Hill fort
Cemetery

Harkerside
Moor

Cogden
Gill

Cogden
Hall

Grovebeck
Gill

Hut & level

Ridley
Hush

Smelt
Mill

Flue

Grovebeck Mining
Grounds

Blenk's
Hush

Grinton How Hill
Mining Grounds

THE WALK

1. From the green follow the road back towards Richmond and cross the bridge over the Arkle Beck, then follow the pavement on the right side of the road and two hundred metres after the bridge leave the roadside to turn right through a small gate that has a footpath signpost next to it. Follow the path alongside the beck and then, after passing the farm, when it turns away, follow it through the fields to exit out onto the road next to Grinton Bridge. **GR 046 985.**

2. At the road turn right to cross the bridge over the Swale and enter Grinton. Hard as it may be, walk past the pub and just after, the main road turns sharply left follow it round.

As you pass the Bridge Inn, St Andrew's Church lies on the right side of the road. Known as the 'Cathedral of the Dales' it's history goes back to Norman times although much of the building, including the nave and chancel are 15th century. In the past a 'curfew bell' used to be rung from the church to guide travellers lost on the moors back to Grinton. It was sounded every minute between eight and quarter past eight on the dark nights from 25 October until 25 March with the exception of Sunday nights. Presumably you had no business being out on the moors on the night of the Sabbath !!

Follow the pavement on the left side of the road through the village and out the other side to come to the cemetery. Immediately after the cemetery there is a stile over the wall on the left. Cross and turn right to follow a permissive path alongside the wall on the right.

Before you start following the wall though, let your eyes follow the line of the cemetery wall straight ahead to see the small hill in front. This is the small

The earthworks of the hill-fort at the bottom of the cemetery.

85

glacial moraine seen from the other side of the river on Walk 3, from here the earthworks that make up the Iron Age settlement can be clearly seen.

Follow the line of the wall, with the road on the opposite side, until you come to the end of the field where you will find a gate that exits back out onto the road. **GR 054 981**.

3. Go through the gate and cross the road, bearing slightly to the right, to the entrance of Cogden Hall where there is a bridleway sign pointing up the track. Head up the track and ignore the small gate and footpath sign on the right, to come to a track junction next to some barns. Turn right onto the side track and follow it as it bears to the left between the barns and once past the older, stone buildings, starts to climb the side of the hill.

As you climb the imposing building of Cogden Hall comes into view on the left. Built in the late 1700's for the Lord of the Manor of East Grinton, the hall probably stands on the site of an earlier fortified building.

Pass through a gate and then the track curves round to the right to pass beneath a small wood. Stay on the track as it makes it's way above Cogden Gill on the right and passes though three fields of rough pasture. In the last field there is a

Climbing up beneath the small wood.

junction with a faint track heading off to the left but continue straight ahead making for the distinctive shape of Sharrow Hill in front and a gate leading onto the roadside. **GR 052 969**.

4. Cross straight over the road to follow a clear path as it continues climbing and curves round to the right to pass under the rock outcrops of Sharrow Hill. As it goes round the side of the hill the path passes a number of disused bell pits on the right and an unusual three-arched lime kiln on the left, normally lime kilns are single or double-arched.

Sharrow Hill is a limestone bluff which makes it a handy place for a quarry and a set of kilns. The name comes from the Old English words 'scearu' and 'hoh', meaning the heel shaped hill on the boundary.

A rather occupied lime kiln.

Shortly after passing the lime kiln, the path comes to the very distinctive remains of the old flue from Grinton Smelt Mill running up the side of the hill from the valley below. **GR 051 965**.

5. For those that are interested, it is fairly easy going to turn left here and follow the flue up to the edge of the moor where a now vanished chimney released the toxic fumes from the smelt mill into the atmosphere. However the route of the walk is to turn right and follow the path of the flue down into the valley to the well preserved remains of Grinton Smelt Mill. **GR 049 964**. See the feature on Grinton How Smelt Mill.

6. From the smelt mill turn left to follow the water channel upstream and come to the remains of the earth banked dam that formed a small reservoir. Just past the dam a well-made track lies on the opposite bank of the stream. Cross the shallow ford over the water and head up this track as it starts to climb the opposite side of the valley. As you climb keep remembering to look behind you for some spectacular views of the old smelt mill and the flue snaking it's way up the hillside. As the track rises, a highly visible area of old mine workings and spoil heaps can be seen in front although at one point the track seems to head away, it does curve back to go right through them.

These are the start of the mining grounds of the Grinton How Mine, probably named after the nearby How Hill where the lead vein was first discovered. From here the vein, called the How Vein surprisingly enough, ran in a line up to the Height of Greets and was worked throughout it's length. As with most mining grounds a combination of methods were used to access the ore, hushing, levels and shafts.

Approaching the Grinton How Mine workings.

The mine was one of the earliest in this part of Swaledale being worked during the 17th century and in 1650 was valued at £6. The most productive period of it's life was between 1696 and 1736 with the higher section close to Height of Greets yielding the largest volume of ore.

By the 1750's output from the mine had started to decline but a short revival at the southern end of the vein led to Blenk's, shown on the OS map as How Hush, and Ridley's Hushes being opened. How Level was driven from the point where Blenk's and Ridley's hushes joined in order to access deeper levels of the vein than could be reached by hushing and was probably started around the 1820's. The level was driven for one mile under the hill but although some ore was produced, this enterprise was not a great success and by 1867 work had stopped. After over two hundred years of production, work on the How Vein ceased.

As you pass through the workings you'll come to the remains of an upright wall, rather like a gable end, and here, if you head over to the right you'll come to the source of all these spoil heaps. A short distance from the track lies the path of a hush and if you follow the water course you'll come to a level entrance from which the stream flows.

The level entrance at the bottom of the hushes.

On the left of the level entrance a well-walked path follows the line of the hush. After a short distance you'll come to where the hush forks left and right, this is actually the junction of two separate hushes, Blenk's Hush on the left and Ridley Hush on the right. The path follows the line of the left hand hush, making it's way through the stones lining the bottom of this small man-made valley. Continue following the hush up the side of the hill until you come to the side of the road. **GR 038 962.**

As you walk up this narrow, steep-sided hush imagine what it was like two hundred years ago. The stones and rocks beneath your feet are wet and glistening from the torrent of water that has been released from the dam high on the moor above you and which has cut it's way down through the hush. As you make your way through the left-over pools of water and try to keep your footing on the loose rocks, the pick and other tools that you carry form a heavy weight on your back and shoulders. Then, along with your workmates, you reach the work face. Six to eight hours of hard, manual labour now follow, heaving pick and shovel against the rock to bring out the ore. The noise, the dirt, the dust and the smell, the working conditions being only marginally better than being down a mine itself. But working in a mine, to an extent, pro-

89

tected you from the elements, the workers on the open cast as we would call it today, worked throughout the year in all conditions. In winter when the water froze in the leats and couldn't be directed down the hush and summer when the heat enveloped the workings in dust and the enclosed space made the air stifling, no matter the conditions you and your mates worked or your families went hungry. Water power is credited with creating these scars on the landscape which undoubtedly they are but in reality even though water was a vital factor, the major part of all these deep gashes was created by the hard physical graft of the human arm and back.

Walking up How Hush.

7. Turn right to follow the road downhill for approximately 500 metres until it bends sharply to the right and here you'll find a bridleway signpost on the left side of the road pointing the way down a sunken track. **GR 039 964**.

8. Turn left to leave the road and make your way down the sunken track and after a short distance come to a well-made vehicle track. Turn left onto the track and follow it, soon you'll come to a fence and gate, pass through and continue on the track. As you make your way along, a shooting hut and a large spoil heap will become visible in the distance. The track curves it's way towards the hut and as you get closer the sources of the spoil heap appear alongside the track, hushes carved into the side of the hill and old pits identified by the characteristic

Approaching the shooting hut and spoil heaps at Grovebeck.

The level entrance.

donut shape of earth. However, it is only when you get to the hut that the main source of the spoil is identified, hidden behind the hut is the entrance to the mine level from which the bulk of the spoil was extracted. Continue on the main track as it bears right round the side of the spoil heap, ignoring the minor track that heads off to the left. After a short distance it will cross a stream and turn to the right, ignore the path on the bend corner and continue on the main track. After a while you'll come to a track junction. **GR 033 972**.

9. Go straight ahead following the track as it continues to head downhill. Eventually a wall will appear on the right and the track will start to follow it. Pass through a gate and then both track and wall bend to the right to come to another gate that leads onto the roadside opposite Bleak House. **GR 032 983**.

10. Cross the road and go through the gate on the left side of the building and then follow the grassy path that curves round the back of the house and de-

Following the track down Harkerside with Reeth in the background.

scends the hill behind. At the bottom of the bank and slightly to the right, can be seen a barn that has had better days. Head down to it and go through the red gate at the right of the buildings. Then turn left to go round the side of the barn and make for a stile half way down the wall on the right. This is a real "squeeze" stile so go through it, making sure that you don't leave any of your bits on the wall, and then head diagonally across the next field making for the small wicket gate to the left of the cottage. Pass through and go across the narrow field to the gate opposite. Here you'll find yourself at the top of the bank looking over the river below. Head down the bank making for the single tree next to the fence to come to a stile over the wire. Once across, turn right to follow the path over to the swing bridge and when there, cross and bear right to follow the same paths that you have used previously to get back to Reeth.

Grinton How Smelt Mill and it's flue.

GRINTON HOW SMELT MILL

It is not known when the first mill alongside Cogden Beck was built but is thought to be in the early 1700's and is certainly shown on a map of the Manor of Grinton that was made in 1768. This map shows a single building with a chimney at the south end and a separate building as the peat store. There were also two reservoirs to supply the water for the water wheel.

The mill was situated in an ideal position on the banks of the beck. The waters of the Cogden provided a regular and constant supply for the processing of the ore. Fuel for the mill was provided from the nearby Coal Pit Moor where coal was extracted from bell pits and peat was readily available from the moor itself. Located just below the hill, the development of the lead vein that ran from there to Height of Greets gave it plenty of ore to process.

The mill remained in this format until 1820/22 when it was extensively rebuilt and the distinctive flue added. By 1888 the mill had two scotch hearths, a slag hearth, roasting furnace, and three water wheels. In 1895 the company that

Looking at the smelt mill and peat store from the banks of the old reservoir.

owned the mill at the time, The Grinton Mining & Smelting Co Ltd, was officially dissolved and that meant the end of smelting at the mill.

However, the end of lead smelting did not mean the demise of the buildings and they continued being used albeit for more agricultural purposes. The peat house being used for storing hay and as an animal shelter while the mill itself was used to house a sheep dip. These uses remain to this day with the casual visitor often encountering sheep in the buildings. This complex of mill buildings are one of the last instances of smelting mills surviving relatively intact to the present day, very probably due to this continued use of the buildings instead of abandoning them as happened on most sites. What can be seen now is a complex comprised of a T-shaped smelt mill, a rectangular peat store, a stone flue that runs from the mill up the side of Sharrow hill, a dam and reservoir, the foundations of the old smithy and a series of track ways. Over recent years a number of information boards have been placed by the National Park Authority within the mill.

The mill and the peat store lie next to each other but on two narrow terraces, partially natural and partially man-made, with the peat store being on the higher of the two levels. The flue left the mill at a fairly high level up the wall, about the same height as the peat store terrace, and then ran along the south side of the store, under the main track and up the side of Sharrow Hill to a small chimney now no longer standing. The total length of the flue being 333 metres (1,100 feet).

The large open doors on the peat store helped air circulate and dry out the peat after it was gathered on the moors.

To the south east of the mill lies a low earth and stone bank which dammed the stream to create a small, triangular reservoir. The dam wall is not particularly high, only about 1 metre above the present water level but has a length of 32 metres. It is partially breached which allows the waters of the stream to flow through.

Downstream of the dam the water enters a culverted section where the banks of the stream are lined with dressed sandstone blocks. This allowed a level working area to be created on the ground surrounding the mill.

The water channel leading from the old reservoir.

In between the mill and the dam a low pile of stones marks the location of a two storey building. Marked as a 'smithy' on early maps, this may have been a blacksmith's shop and/or offices and stores.

Within the mill building some of the original timber fixtures can still be seen. The bellows room contains a large timber frame which supported the bellows, a mechanically operated method of supplying blasts of air to help increase the temperature in the furnaces. This room also has a wooden water channel high above the room floor, this is a launder and provided water for a water wheel at the side of the building which is now long gone.

Descending down into Apedale.

WALK 9: HARKERSIDE & APEDALE

Swaledale is closely tied with lead mining although most people tend to associate it with the northern side of the valley such as Gunnerside Gill, the Old Gang Mines and the mines in Arkengarthdale. However, the lead seams flowed on both sides of the valley and this walk covers a wide expanse of mining ground throughout the length of it's entire route including the small, isolated valley of Apedale which in it's heyday was a hive of mining activity. But don't think that this walk is all about the after effects of lead as on a good day, it will give you some of the best views in the whole of Swaledale with an extensive panorama down the length of the dale to the high Pennines that separate it from the Eden Valley on the western side of the watershed.

Harkerside is a large area of land sloping down to the southern banks of the Swale. The name comes from the Old Norse 'akr' meaning an acre or open field. This indicates that during the time of the Viking settlement of the dale, that far from being the open moor of today that this was a cultivated area with the main crop probably being oats, oatmeal being the staple food of the time.

DISTANCE: 9.9 miles (15.8 km)
ASCENT: 1,614 feet (492 metres)

TERRAIN: The route is all on track, the majority of which is well-surfaced vehicle track although descending down from Height of Greets, the track does become more of a grass track and in places can be a bit boggy especially after wet weather. With the route being on vehicle track, the hills tend to be long, gradual climbs rather than steep.

TIME: 5 to 6 hours.

START: Car parking space at the junction of the Redmire and Leyburn roads above Grinton. GR SE 046 978

DOGS: As the route is all on rights of way then dogs are allowed. However, as the route also goes through a number of mining grounds where there are old shafts, levels and holes in the ground, then you may need to keep them under very close control. Sheep will be encountered throughout the route.

ACCESS: This route is all on public rights of way although in certain places the tracks followed do not exactly match the right of way but as this area is all open access land then this should not present any problems.

Grid references:

Parking space	046 978
Road/track junction	044 974
Track crossroads	033 972
Track junction	012 973
Track junction	987 958
Track crossroads	030 942
Height of Greets	028 956
Track/road junction	038 963
Parking space	046 978

FGS Grading
Grading is F6 [D1, N1, T0, R2, H2]

Distance	1	6 – 12 miles
Navigation	1	Basic navigation skills needed
Terrain	0	75% + on graded track or path
Remoteness	2	Countryside not in close proximity to habitation – less than 20% of the route within 2 miles
Height	2	Over 125 ft per mile

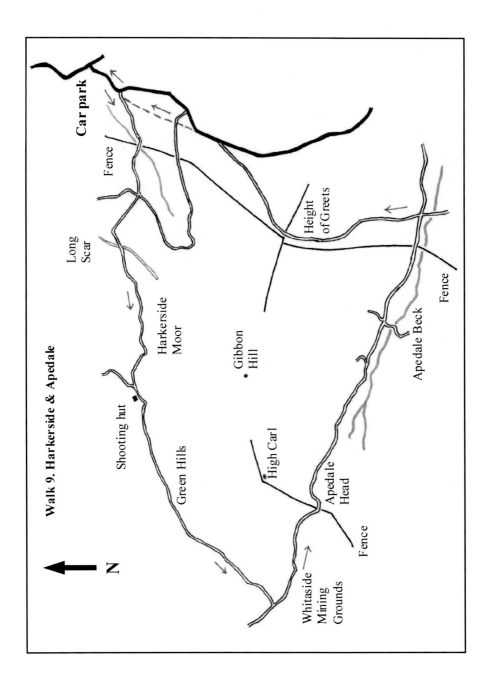

Walk 9. Harkerside & Apedale

Car park

Fence

Long Scar

Harkerside Moor

Gibbon Hill

Shooting hut

Green Hills

High Carl

Apedale Head

Whitaside Mining Grounds

Fence

Apedale Beck

Fence

Height of Greets

N

THE WALK

1. From the parking space turn right to follow the Redmire Road steeply uphill for 400/500 metres passing as you do a footpath signpost and a bridleway, the post for this one being on the left side of the road directing the bridleway across it. When you come to a sharp left hand bend in the road you'll find a second bridleway post, this time on the right side of the road, pointing up a track. **GR 044 974.**

2. Leave the road and follow this track as it heads towards a distant Low Harker Hill. The OS map shows a number of paths and bridleways crossing this track but stay on the obvious main track to come to a gate and a couple of metres after this, a stream crossing.

The stream is the Grovebeck Gill after which it is thought that the lead mines in this area are named, see Walk 8. However, there is always the possibility that the stream was named after the mines. Groove is an old North Country word for a mine, probably coming from the Old Norse word meaning 'to dig'. Following from this, miners themselves were known as 'groovers'. At their height there were three smelt mills along this gill processing the ore produced by the mines and the area around the stream was used for the processing of lead ore, as you climb up the small bank on the other side of the stream the earth bank retaining wall of a small reservoir is just metres away from the left side of the track.

The earth bank wall of the old reservoir.

Continue on the track to come to a crossroads of tracks. **GR 033 972**.

3. At the crossroads continue on the track ahead that climbs up Low Harker Hill. As you reach the shoulder of the hill you'll pass Long Scar, marked by two cairns on the left of the track. The girdle of stones running round the brow of the hill marking Long Scar is the remnants of one of the Dark Age dyke and ditch defensive systems that blocked the entrance to the upper valley. See the feature on the Grinton - Fremington Dykes.

The dyke of Long Scar.

Stay on the main track as it bends to the left to run over the shoulder of the hill before it approaches an area of old lead workings where it starts to descend. *These are the grounds of the Harkerside Mines, the first indicator of which is the long deep hush running along the left side of the track for a distance of over 800 metres (half a mile) as it crosses the saddle of High Harker Hill. Work had started on these mines very early and they had proved to be highly productive, by 1650 it was valued at £20 per annum, a significant sum for the day. However by 1768 the veins were becoming exhausted and although it was worked on a dwindling scale, it's best years were behind it. Not long after, the mines were left idle and were finally abandoned between 1800 and 1861.*

As well as this hush, a number of shafts were also sunk and at least two levels driven into the hillside. Over on the north or dale side of the hill more ore was extracted using hushes, the scars of which you'll see as you pass by.

The track now runs across the side of the hill again giving some superb views up the length of the valley to the high hills of the Pennines that block in the far end

The view up the dale from the track.

of the dale. Eventually you'll come to a junction with a track on the right. **GR 012 973**.

4. Continue straight on at the junction making for a shooting hut in front and after you have passed that, the track bends to the left to cross the seasonal stream of Browna Gill.

Even at this point the area is not free of lead workings, 200 metres up from the ford lies the level of the Brownagill Mines. The shafts themselves lying further up on the top of the hill.

The track now makes for Green Hill Ends where it bends to the left to climb the short distance up Green Hill and once there passes the stonework of an old lime kiln on the right. This lime kiln is a bit of an oddity as it seems to have been built in the remains of an old hush, perhaps utilising the stone removed during the hushing process. Stay on the track as it curves round the side of the hill. Eventually a group of spoil heaps come into view and once you reach them you'll come to a track junction. **GR 987 958**.

As you approach the spoil heaps, this is the first evidence that you are entering the Whitaside mining grounds even though the track has been passing through them since Greena Hill. The Whitaside Mines are some of the oldest in Swaledale and were also some of the most productive. Part of the workings on Far Greena Hill are documented in a will dating back to 1504.

However, the main mines follow a line of veins and small veins, known as strings, from below the hamlet of Crackpot up to the Wensleydale boundary where the mining grounds of the Apedale Head Mine begins. The track, as it turns left at the junction next to the spoil heaps, runs through the mining ground with evidence of old shafts and hushes on either side. At one point the track even has to bend to the right as it passes over the side of one of the shafts. Shown as Morley's Folly on the OS map, this shaft is more correctly called Morley's Shaft being named after one of the Morley family who, in partnership with others, held the mining leases for the Whitaside field.

At their height, in 1768, the Whitaside mines employed 400 people, around 100 of which were women and children who were employed to dress and sort the ore, fetch and carry and other menial jobs. However, because of the volatility of the lead industry by 1775, a mere seven years later, this number of workers was down to 80.

As with all mines, the fortunes of Whitaside went up and down and work continued on them for another one hundred years with various levels of employment. The mine finally closed around 1889 ending what may have been over 400 years of lead mining in this ore field.

5. Turn left at the junction and follow the track as it climbs up through the old mine workings, following an old hush on the right side. As you get to the top of the moor the track forms the only piece of solid ground as it makes it's way

The track making it's way through the mine workings.

through the peat hags but even amongst these there lies the remains of old shafts and workings. As you reach the summit of the moor a fence line comes into view that marks Apedale Head. Pass through the gate in the fence and you now start the 3 km descent down and along the isolated valley of Apedale. The track makes a steady descent down into the valley passing numerous old shafts and hushes along the way. After just over 1 km, all of a sudden the track descends quite steeply while it negotiates the gash produced by a hush coming in from the right hand side.

Here the track crosses over the top of one of the many levels driven into the sides of this valley, if you step off the left side of the track the characteristic stone arch of the level entrance is clearly seen as it cuts through underneath the hush.

The entrance of the level lying underneath the track.

The track continues down and as it rounds the side of the hill, below you can be seen a number of wooden beams laid against the side of the hill. These beams hide the entrance to a second level, which again, the track runs over. The track now crosses an old bridge and meets a second track going up the side of the hill on the left but stay on the valley floor track. The flat area between the track and the beck used to be a large dressing floor where the ore was processed before being taken to the smelt mill. Take the time to have a look and you'll see a number of earth banks with the ground being split into different levels marking the different parts of the process. The track now runs along the floor of the narrow valley and you'll soon see another track running down from the right. This track joins onto yours in front of a large flat area that contains a number of spoil heaps. Hidden up to now by the spoil heaps, there is also a junction with another track here, this time on the left.

The flat area in front was a major processing site as can be seen from the amount of spoil. Hidden amongst the visible wall remains is the stone-lined trough of a water wheel pit, The waterwheel being the power house that drove the ore crushing machinery.

Stay on the track as it passes a number of hushes and shafts on the left side to come, after 800 metres, to a gate in a fence. Pass through the gate and continue the short distance to come to a crossroads of tracks next to a small stone building and tin shed, the buildings of Dent's Houses lie a short distance away on the right. **GR 030 942**.

Approaching Dent's Houses and the track crossroads.

Now unpopulated, the isolated valley of Apedale had during the 18th century at least four houses holding an unknown number of inhabitants. However, this was a sizeable community in it's own right with the parish registers recording several births here.

6. Turn left at the crossroads and follow this track up the side of the hill not forgetting, the higher you get, to look back behind you for some lovely views over the hills of Wensleydale. As you climb you'll come to a track junction where you follow the right branch, the left just takes you into an old disused quarry. After another few hundred metres you'll approach the fence line running over the summit of Height of Greets. (**GR 028 956**). Pass through the gate to the right

Looking down onto the Grinton How mining ground from the cairn on Heights of Greets.

of the summit cairn and continue following the track as it runs on the right of the fence. After a short distance the track bears to the right away from the fence line and becomes more of a grass track as it makes it's way between the old workings. The track will soon come to a row of grouse butts and here divides. It actually doesn't matter which branch you take as they both join the road that can be seen a short distance away, just one joining it slightly higher up than the other. The higher branch arriving at the road at **GR 038 963**.

7. Turn left onto the road and follow it down the hill until it takes a sharp turn to the right and here leave it on the left hand side to follow a sunken path shown by a bridleway. After a short distance the path comes to a well-made vehicle track. Cross over this and to the left of the concrete pond is both a continuation of the sunken path and a grassy track. The grassy track is the better walking and as they both arrive at the same point, the top of a row of grouse butts, then it makes more sense to use the track. When you get to the grouse butts follow the path down the side of them to come to another well-made vehicle track. This is the same track that you left the road on at the beginning of the walk, so now turn right to follow it for the 200 metres back to the road and then turn left to follow the road back to the car.

APPENDIX

Ferguson Grading System (`FGS`)

1. Introduction

The FGS has been adopted as a means of assessing the nature and severity of the various walks in this book and the abilities and equipment needed to tackle each one safely. The FGS was developed by Stuart Ferguson, a long time fell and trail runner, climber, mountaineer, mountain-biker and general outdoor enthusiast. In the opinion of Trailguides, the FGS is the most accurate and comprehensive grading system for comparing off-road walking, running and mountain-biking routes anywhere in the country.

2. The System

Tables 1 & 2, set out below, are used in order to give a grading to each route. Table 1 sets out three categories of country that a route could potentially cross, together with a range of factors that would need to be considered when tackling that route. The three categories are, Trail, Fell and Mountain, and after assessing which category best fits the route, a letter, either `T`, `F` or `M`, is allocated to that route. Where a route does not fit perfectly into one of the three categories the closest category is allocated.

Table 2 deals with five specific aspects of the route, namely distance, navigation, terrain, remoteness and height gain, and each one is allocated a letter, `D`, `N`, `T`, `R`, and `H`. Each letter is also given a severity score from the range 0-3 or 0-4, in respect of distance (`D`). The higher the number, the more severe the route. The five severity scores are then added together to give an overall score. The overall score is then put with the Table 1 category letter (i.e. `T`, `F` or `M`).

In order to show how the grading has been determined for each walk in this book, the five individual severity scores are set out, in square brackets, immediately after the actual grading. So, for example, Walk 1 Hurst has a grading of F6 [D1, N1, T1, R1, H2], indicating that it is a Fell Category walk with a total severity score of 6. This is made up of the five specific severity scores, for distance (`D`), navigation (`N`), terrain (`T`), remoteness (`R`) and height gain (`H`), of 1, 1, 1, 1 and 2 respectively. The highest total severity score which can be achieved is 16 and the lowest total severity score achievable is 0.

The table which accompanies the grading for each walk sets out the specific factors, extracted from Table 2, that need to be considered when tackling that particular walk.

TABLE 1

	TRAIL	FELL	MOUNTAIN
Description	Lowland and forest areas including urban, cultivated and forested locations.	Moorlands and upland areas which may include some upland cultivated and forestry areas plus possibly remote locations.	Upland and mountain areas including remote and isolated locations.
Height	Not usually above 1,000 feet but may go up to 2,500 feet	Usually above 1,000 feet, up to 2,500 feet and above.	Usually above 2,500 feet and up to 4,000 feet.
Way-marking	Usually	Limited	None
Terrain	Usually graded paths, tracks and trails but may include some off-trail	May include some graded paths, tracks and trails but mainly off-trail	Virtually all off-trail
Height gain	Limited height gain	May include considerable height gain	May include some severe height gain.
Effects of weather	Very limited effect	May be prone to sudden weather changes	Extreme weather a possibility
Navigational skills	None to basic	Basic to competent	Competent to expert
Equipment	Walking shoes/boots. Possibly waterproofs Food and drink dependant upon route.	3/4 season walking boots. Full waterproof cover. Possibly map and compass dependant upon route. Food and drink dependant upon route.	Mountain boots. Full waterproof cover. Map and compass. Food and drink
Escape Routes	Yes	Some	Some to nil

TABLE 2

Score	0	1	2	3	4
Distance	Up to 6 miles	6 – 12 miles	12 – 18 miles	18 miles +	24 miles +
Navigation	No navigation skills needed	Basic navigation skills needed	Competent navigation skills needed	Expert navigation skills needed	
Terrain	75% + on graded track or path	50 – 75% on graded track or path 25 – 50% off track	25 -50% on graded track or path 50 – 75% off track	Under 25% on graded track or path Over 75% off track	
Remoteness	Urban	Countryside in fairly close proximity to habitation – at least 80% of the route within 2 miles	Countryside not in close proximity to habitation – less than 20% of the route within 2 miles	Remote, isolated location	
Height gain	Less than 100 ft per mile	Over 100 ft per mile	Over 125 ft per mile	Over 250 ft per mile	

Notes to Table 2

Graded paths = Well established paths with a stable surface.

Escape routes = The opportunity to cut the route short and return to the start without completing the full course in the event of weather changes or unforeseen incidents.

The Author

Keven Shevels

Kev has been involved with outdoor sports since his school days doing the Duke of Edinburgh award, spending his time either walking or running and latterly mountain biking through the countryside of the Northern Dales and beyond. He first went up Swaledale as a young lad with his father, the pair of them fishing on the Swale above Grinton. In his teens he did all his training for and his actual Duke of Edinburgh expedition on the hills above Muker and Gunnerside and then during his twenties and thirties when he was heavily into fell running, one of his must-do events each year was the Swaledale Marathon, starting from Reeth and covering the moors between there and Gunnerside.

As you can guess he's always liked this part of the world and over the years both the history and the landscape of the dale have held a fascination for him. His great delight is spending hours reading a map and coming up with new routes which he can then subsequently set forth to explore. This in-built curiosity to go and view things, more often than not, leads him to objects and places that don't appear in other guide books and he enjoys sharing these experiences with those that read his ramblings.

Now in his fifties, Kev has been unable to continue his running due to injury problems but that hasn't curtailed his pleasure from being in the great outdoors and he now spends as much of his time as he can walking the hills and dales of this region. Over the last couple of years he has been the co-author of one of the most innovative series of coaching books for fell and trail runners published and he now brings his easy to read, informative style of writing to guide books for those who walk in the countryside of the Northern Dales.

Trailguides Limited

Trailguides is a small independent publisher specialising in publications for those who enjoy the great outdoors. Our target is to produce guides that are as user-friendly and informative as possible and all in an easily readable format. In essence, to increase the enjoyment of the user and to showcase the very best of the great British countryside. Our series of books explores the heritage of us all and lets you see our landscape with new eyes. These books are written to not just take you on a walk but to investigate, explore and understand the objects, places and history that has shaped not just the land but also the people of this country.

If you've enjoyed following the routes in this guide and want news and details of other publications that are being developed by Trailguides then look at the company website at **www.trailguides.co.uk**

Comments and, yes, criticisms, are always welcomed especially if you discover a change to a route. Contact us by email through the website or by post at Trailguides Limited, 35 Carmel Road South, Darlington, Co Durham DL3 8DQ.

Other walking books from Trailguides.
At the time of publication the following books are also available but with new titles being regularly added to our publication list keep checking our website.

Northumberland.
The Cheviot Hills.
Walks from Wooler.
The Hills of Upper Coquetdale.
Walks from Kirknewton.
Walks Around Rothbury and Coquetdale.
Walks on the Wild Side: The Cheviot Hills.

County Durham.
Hamsterley Forest.
The Barningham Trail.
Ancient Stones.
The High Hills of Teesdale.
Walks from Stanhope.
Mid-Teesdale Walks.

North Yorkshire.
The Hills of Upper Swaledale.

Walks around Gunnerside.
Walks around Reeth and Upper Swaledale.

Walking North East.

Visit our website and sign up to receive our free newsletter, Walking North East, dedicated to walking in North Eastern England. Full of news, views and articles relating to this the forgotten corner of England.

Acknowledgements.

Are due to Harry Manuel for accompanying me on these walks and helping with the route testing and occasionally appearing as the "model" in some of the photographs. Thanks are also due to my wife Lyn for the patience and tolerance shown while I "disappear" to walk and write about these routes.

I'd also like to give my gratitude and thanks to a group of people, who quite frankly don't know me from Adam. These are the archaeologists and historians, who over the years have made a study of the dale's past of which I have been an avid reader for most of my life. Although I have not deliberately set out to plagiarise, I cannot deny the influence and knowledge that I have gained from reading the works of Arthur Raistrick, Tim Laurie, Andrew Fleming and others. Their work has often opened my eyes to the landscape and provided the inspiration behind a walk whether as a route for a book or just purely for pleasure and for that I am grateful.